60 Recipes for Apache CloudStack

Sébastien Goasguen

Beijing · Cambridge · Farnham · Köln · Sebastopol · Tokyo

60 Recipes for Apache CloudStack

by Sébastien Goasguen

Copyright © 2014 Sébastien Goasguen. All rights reserved.

Printed in the United States of America.

Published by O'Reilly Media, Inc., 1005 Gravenstein Highway North, Sebastopol, CA 95472.

O'Reilly books may be purchased for educational, business, or sales promotional use. Online editions are also available for most titles (*http://safaribooksonline.com*). For more information, contact our corporate/institutional sales department: 800-998-9938 or *corporate@oreilly.com*.

Editor: Brian Anderson
Production Editor: Matthew Hacker
Copyeditor: Jasmine Kwityn
Proofreader: Linley Dolby

Indexer: Ellen Troutman Zaig
Cover Designer: Karen Montgomery
Interior Designer: David Futato
Illustrator: Rebecca Demarest

September 2014:   First Edition

Revision History for the First Edition:

2014-08-22:   First release

See *http://oreilly.com/catalog/errata.csp?isbn=9781491910139* for release details.

ISBN: 978-1-491-91013-9

[LSI]

Table of Contents

Preface... vii

Part I.   Installation

1. Installing from Source... 3
1.1. Installing the Prerequisites for Ubuntu 14.04   3
1.2. Installing the Prerequisites for CentOS 6.5   4
1.3. Installing from Source   6
1.4. Using the CloudStack Simulator   7
1.5. Using the CloudStack Sandbox: DevCloud   9
1.6. Vagrant-Based CloudStack Testing Deployment   11
1.7. Building CloudStack Binary Packages   13

2. Installing from Packages.. 15
2.1. Installing the Prerequisites on the Management Server   17
2.2. Setting Up the Management Server   19
2.3. Setting Up an Image Catalog and Seeding it with the SystemVM Template   21
2.4. Preparing a KVM Hypervisor   22
2.5. Configuring libvirt   24
2.6. Basic Zone Network Configuration and NAT Router Setup   25
2.7. Configuring a Basic Zone   27
2.8. Troubleshooting Your First CloudStack Deployment   30

Part II.   Clients and API Wrappers

3. API Clients.. 35
3.1. The CloudStack API   35
3.2. Signing an API Request   37

3.3. Installing CloudMonkey, the CloudStack Interactive Shell   39
3.4. Configuring CloudMonkey   40
3.5. Using CloudMonkey as an Interactive Shell   42
3.6. Starting a Virtual Machine Instance with CloudMonkey   43
3.7. Using Apache Libcloud with CloudStack   45
3.8. Managing Key Pairs and Security Groups Using Libcloud   48
3.9. Hybrid Cloud Applications Using Libcloud   49
3.10. IPython Interactive Shell with Libcloud   50
3.11. Installing and Configuring jclouds CLI   51
3.12. Using jclouds CLI with CloudStack   54
3.13. Using CloStack: A Clojure Client for CloudStack   55
3.14. Starting a Virtual Machine with CloStack   59
3.15. Use CloStack Within Your Own Clojure project   60
3.16. StackerBee, a Ruby Client for CloudStack   62

4. API Interfaces. 65
4.1. Installing and Configuring EC2Stack   65
4.2. Using the AWS CLI with EC2Stack   66
4.3. Improving the EC2Stack API Coverage   68
4.4. Using Python Boto with EC2Stack   69
4.5. Installing Eutester to Test the AWS Compatibility of Your CloudStack
Cloud   71
4.6. Using Eutester with EC2Stack to Write Functional tests   72
4.7. Installing and Configuring gstack: The CloudStack GCE Interface   74
4.8. Using gstack with the gcutil Tool   75
4.9. Supporting the OCCI Standard in CloudStack   80

Part III.   Configuration Management and Advanced Recipes

5. Configuration Management. 85
5.1. Installing Veewee   86
5.2. Using Veewee to Create a Vagrant Base Box   86
5.3. Introducing Packer to Build Cloud Images   88
5.4. Installing Vagrant to Build and Test Cloud Images   90
5.5. Using the Vagrant CloudStack Plug-In   92
5.6. Introducing Ansible to Configure Cloud Instances   95
5.7. Provisioning with Ansible Playbooks   97
5.8. Ansible Provisioning with Vagrant CloudStack Plug-In   99
5.9. Installing knife-cloudstack   102
5.10. Starting an Instance with Knife   104
5.11. Bootstrapping Instances with Hosted Chef   105

6. Advanced Recipes.. 109
    6.1. Installing Fluentd to Collect CloudStack Logs and Events   109
    6.2. Configuring the CloudStack Fluentd Plug-In   110
    6.3. Using MongoDB as a Fluent Data Store   113
    6.4. Playing with Basho Riak CS Object Store   115
    6.5. Installing RiakCS on Ubuntu 12.04   117
    6.6. Using Python Boto to Store Data in RiakCS   118
    6.7. Using RiakCS as Secondary Storage for CloudStack   120
    6.8. Installing Apache Whirr   123
    6.9. Using Apache Whirr to Deploy a Hadoop Cluster   124

Part IV. Summary

7. Summary.. 129
    What We Covered   129
    Other Areas to Explore   130
    Final Words   131

Index.. 133

Preface

If you are a CloudStack user, you should read this book! If you are a CloudStack developer, you should read this book! If you are a DevOps-minded person, you should read this book! If you are an application developer, you should read this book! This might sound like a joke, but this is really the intent. This book covers the Apache CloudStack ecosystem, but it also introduces tools that are used in different setups. For example, we'll take a look at tools such as Chef, Ansible, and Vagrant, as well as applications (e.g., Hadoop) and storage solutions (e.g., RiakCS). This is much more than just CloudStack.

This is not a standard cookbook with multiple recipes on a single topic. It covers a variety of tools and provides introductory material for each. It is meant to be used as a reference that you can open at any time for a quick tutorial on how to use a specific tool or application so that you can make effective use of it. Used in combination with CloudStack, these tools are becoming core technologies used by developers, system administrators, and architects alike. They build on the foundation of a solid cloud and empower IT professionals to do things better and faster.

Why I Wrote This Book

I have been working with virtualization and what became known as clouds since around 2002. If we want to build a cloud, we now have several open source solutions, which Marten Mickos, CEO of Eucalyptus, has called the four sisters: CloudStack, Eucalyptus (*https://www.eucalyptus.com/*), OpenNebula (*http://opennebula.org/*), and OpenStack (*http://www.openstack.org/*). Successful private and public clouds are currently operational all over the world using these solutions, so it appears that *building a cloud* is now a solved problem. The capabilities of those clouds are certainly different and the scalability of each solution—as well as some specific networking or storage features—might be different, but they are operational and in production. This is why I believe that instead of an installation book, it is important to look at the software ecosystem of those cloud solutions and start thinking about using the cloud, integrating it in the development and operational processes so that we can provide higher level services using this foundation and start getting some return on investment.

Since I joined the Apache CloudStack community in July 2012, I have worked actively to test and, when necessary, develop CloudStack drivers in a lot of tools that make the arsenal of today's IT developer and system administrators. Increasingly, I believe that users can also leverage these tools directly. I wanted to write this book so that I could share my experience with testing these tools and explain how they are relevant to answer the question "I have a cloud, now what?" Then we can get back to focusing on the problems at hand: reliable application hosting, distributed application deployments, data processing, and so on.

The cloud has matured, and this book will show you various tools and techniques to take full advantage of it so that you can stop worrying about the implementation details of your cloud and get back to working on your applications.

CloudStack Within the Cloud Computing Picture in 500 Words

Cloud computing can be a very nebulous term—for some it is an online application, for others it is a virtualization system. To set the record straight, the definition (*http://csrc.nist.gov/publications/nistpubs/800-145/SP800-145.pdf*) put forth by the National Institute for Standards and Technology (NIST) is helpful. In its 2011 report, NIST defined cloud computing as follows:

> Cloud computing is a model for enabling ubiquitous, convenient, on-demand network access to a shared pool of of configurable computing resources (e.g., networks, servers, storage, applications, and services) that can be rapidly provisioned and released with minimal management effort...

The NIST definition goes on to define the essential characteristics of clouds (i.e., on-demand, network access, multitenancy, elasticity, and metering). It continues by defining three service models: software as a service (SaaS), platform as a service (PaaS), and infrastructure as a service (IaaS). It also identifies four deployment models: private cloud, public cloud, hybrid cloud, and community cloud (note that community cloud is a less recognized model and is not commonly used today).

The SaaS to IaaS model can be mapped to the old ISO model. SaaS deals with application delivery, IaaS deals with infrastructure management, and PaaS is everything in between. That's a very simplified view of things, but it's not too far off. SaaS refers to online application hosting: users will access the application interface over the Internet, and all the work that happens in the background to make the application available and scalable is entirely hidden from the end user (as it should be). Gmail (and most Google services, including Calendar and Docs) is a typical SaaS example. PaaS represents what we used to call middleware, and makes the link between the end-user application and the underlying infrastructure that it is running on. A PaaS solution is aimed at developers who do not want to worry about the infrastructure. PaaS is a fast-moving area these days with solutions such as Openshift (*http://www.openshift.com*), CloudFoundry (*http://cloudfoundry.org*), and Cloudify (*http://cloudifysource.org*) receiving a lot of attention and being developed extremely fast. IaaS is the infrastructure layer that orchestrates the work typically done by system administrators to host the applications, including server provisioning, network management, and storage allocation.

Apache CloudStack is an infrastructure as a service (IaaS) software solution. It aims at managing large sets of virtual machine instances in a highly available, highly scalable way. It is used to build public or private clouds to offer on-demand, elastic, multitenant compute, storage, and network services. As mentioned earlier, it is known as one of the four sisters of open source cloud computing that allows you to build an Amazon EC2 clone.

CloudStack's development was begun by a Silicon Valley startup called VMOps (*http://bit.ly/CloudStack_origin*) in 2008. The company was renamed Cloud.com in 2010, and in 2011, Citrix Systems acquired Cloud.com (*http://bit.ly/Cloud_acquisition*). In April 2012, Citrix donated CloudStack to the Apache Software Foundation (ASF) (*http://www.apache.org*). CloudStack then entered the Apache Incubator and became a trademark of the ASF, graduating to become a top-level ASF project (*http://bit.ly/Cloud Stack_graduates*) in March 2013, joining other open source projects like HTTPD and Hadoop.

How This Book Is Organized

To get you up to speed on the Apache CloudStack ecosystem, the book is organized in three parts with two chapters each. Part I discusses installation steps, both from source and from binaries:

- Chapter 1, *Installing from Source* covers some basic installation steps for developers. The CloudStack documentation (*http://docs.cloudstack.apache.org*) provides complete installation instructions, so we will not cover these details here. Instead, this chapter is meant to introduce CloudStack and some features that can help ecosystem development (e.g., the simulator and DevCloud, the CloudStack sandbox).

- Chapter 2, *Installing from Packages* is a step-by-step installation guide for Ubuntu 14.04 using KVM. This guide can be followed on a local machine using VMware fusion (to do nested virtualization with KVM) or on physical hardware. It is intended for users who do not want to compile from source.

Part II discusses API clients and wrappers:

- Chapter 3, *API Clients* explains how to sign an API request and then goes through a few clients, including CloudMonkey (the official CloudStack command-line

interface), Apache Libcloud (a Python module that abstracts the differences between cloud providers' APIs), Apache jclouds (a Java library with a similar goal as
libcloud), and CloStack (a Clojure-based client specific for CloudStack). This chapter should give everyone a taste of a client in their favorite language. This chapter
will be interesting to folks who want to use the CloudStack API and write their own
applications on top of it.

- Chapter 4, *API Interfaces* presents three applications that provide a different API
  in front of the CloudStack API. They are sometimes called API bridges or wrappers.
  These applications run as servers on the user's machine or within the cloud provider
  infrastructure, and expose a different API. For example, EC2Stack exposes an EC2-
  compatible interface, gstack exposes a GCE-compatible interface, and *rOCCI*
  exposes a standardized interface. In addition, this chapter presents Boto and Eutester, two Python modules written by the Eucalyptus team. Boto is a client to Amazon Web Services (AWS) and Eutester is a testing framework. CloudStack users
  will be able to use these modules in combination with EC2Stack.

Part III discusses configuration management and some advanced recipes:

- Chapter 5, *Configuration Management* starts with an introduction to Veewee and
  Packer. Moving on from there, it presents several recipes about Vagrant (*http://
  vagrantup.com*), a software development tool that helps test configurations locally
  and then deploys in the cloud in a repeatable manner. With some knowledge of
  Vagrant, the rest of the chapter is dedicated to the introduction of two configuration
  management solutions, Ansible and Chef. These solutions have CloudStack plug-
  ins that help deploy applications in the cloud. This chapter will be interesting to the
  DevOps community.

- Chapter 6, *Advanced Recipes* goes into some more advanced topics. We look at two
  important aspects of the cloud infrastructure itself: monitoring and storage. We
  introduce RiakCS and show how it can be used as an image catalog. We also show
  how to use Fluent for log aggregation in combination with Elasticsearch and MongoDB. Finally, we introduce Apache Whirr, an application orchestrator built on top
  of jclouds that can be used to deploy and run distributed systems like Hadoop.

Finally, Part IV summarizes the book and provides some tips for further reading and
investigation.

Technology You Need to Understand

This book is of an intermediate level and requires a minimum understanding of a few
development and system administration concepts. Before diving into the book, you
might want to review:

bash (Unix shell)

This is the default Unix shell on Linux and OS X. Familiarity with the Unix shell, such as editing files, setting file permissions, moving files around the filesystems, user privileges, and some basic shell programming will be very beneficial. If you don't know the Linux shell in general, consult books such as Cameron Newham's *Learning the Bash Shell* or Carl Albing, JP Vossen, and Cameron Newham's *bash Cookbook*, both from O'Reilly.

Package management

The tools we will present in this book often have multiple dependencies that need to be met by installing some packages. Knowledge of the package management on your machine is therefore required. It could be `apt` on Ubuntu/Debian systems, `yum` on CentOS/RHEL systems, `port` or `brew` on OS X. Whatever it is, make sure that you know how to install, upgrade, and remove packages.

Git

Git has established itself as the standard for distributed version control. If you are already familiar with CVS and SVN, but have not yet used Git, you should. *Version Control with Git* by Jon Loeliger and Matthew McCullough (O'Reilly) is a good start. Together with Git, the GitHub (*http://github.com*) website is a great resource to get started with a hosted repository of your own. To learn GitHub, try *http://training.github.com* and the associated interactive tutorial (*http://try.github.io*).

Python

In addition to programming with C/C++ or Java, I always encourage students to pick up a scripting language of their choice. Perl used to rule the world, while these days, Ruby and Go seem to be prevalent. I personally use Python. Most examples in this book use Python but there are a few examples with Ruby, one even uses Clojure. O'Reilly offers an extensive collection of books on Python, including *Introducing Python* by Bill Lubanovic, *Programming Python* by Mark Lutz, and *Python Cookbook* by David Beazley and Brian K. Jones.

Those are your weapons: your shell, your package manager, your GitHub account, and some Python. If you don't know these tools (and especially Python), you need not worry. There are recipes for Rubyists and Clojure programmers. You will be able to pick things up as you go along.

Online Content

If you want to take a self-paced training on a few of the tools described in this book, head over to *http://codac.co*, an online tutorial I have presented several times. It makes use of exoscale (*http://exoscale.ch*), a CloudStack-based public cloud. You can register for free on exoscale and you will get free credits that should allow you to go through the tutorial.

Although a lot of the content in this book has been tested on exoscale, there are other public CloudStack clouds that you can use to test these tools and even go to production. You might consider getting an account with any or all of these:

- exoscale (*http://exoscale.ch*)
- iKoula (*http://express.ikoula.com/cloud-public*)
- British Telecom Cloud (*https://www.btcloud.bt.com*)
- GreenQloud (*https://www.greenqloud.com*)
- Leaseweb (*http://www.leaseweb.com/en/cloud*)
- Cloud-n VERIO (*http://www.verio.com/cloud-computing/*)
- PCExtreme (*https://www.pcextreme.nl/en/aurora/*)
- Kuomo (*http://www.kumo.com.co*)
- Interoute Virtual Data Center (VDC) (*http://bit.ly/Interoute_VDC*)

Conventions Used in This Book

The following typographical conventions are used in this book:

Italic
: Indicates new terms, URLs, email addresses, filenames, and file extensions.

`Constant width`
: Used for program listings, as well as within paragraphs to refer to program elements such as variable or function names, databases, data types, environment variables, statements, and keywords.

`Constant width bold`
: Shows commands or other text that should be typed literally by the user.

`Constant width italic`
: Shows text that should be replaced with user-supplied values or by values determined by context.

 This element signifies a tip, suggestion, or general note.

This element indicates a warning or caution.

Safari® Books Online

 *Safari Books Online* is an on-demand digital library that delivers expert content in both book and video form from the world's leading authors in technology and business.

Technology professionals, software developers, web designers, and business and creative professionals use Safari Books Online as their primary resource for research, problem solving, learning, and certification training.

Safari Books Online offers a range of plans and pricing for enterprise, government, education, and individuals.

Members have access to thousands of books, training videos, and prepublication manuscripts in one fully searchable database from publishers like O'Reilly Media, Prentice Hall Professional, Addison-Wesley Professional, Microsoft Press, Sams, Que, Peachpit Press, Focal Press, Cisco Press, John Wiley & Sons, Syngress, Morgan Kaufmann, IBM Redbooks, Packt, Adobe Press, FT Press, Apress, Manning, New Riders, McGraw-Hill, Jones & Bartlett, Course Technology, and hundreds more. For more information about Safari Books Online, please visit us online.

How to Contact Us

Please address comments and questions concerning this book to the publisher:

O'Reilly Media, Inc.
1005 Gravenstein Highway North
Sebastopol, CA 95472
800-998-9938 (in the United States or Canada)
707-829-0515 (international or local)
707-829-0104 (fax)

We have a web page for this book, where we list errata, examples, and any additional information. You can access this page at *http://shop.oreilly.com/product/0636920034377.do*.

To comment or ask technical questions about this book, send email to *bookquestions@oreilly.com*.

For more information about our books, courses, conferences, and news, see our website at *http://www.oreilly.com.*

Find us on Facebook: *http://facebook.com/oreilly*

Follow us on Twitter: *http://twitter.com/oreillymedia*

Watch us on YouTube: *http://www.youtube.com/oreillymedia*

Acknowledgments

Perhaps very strangely, I would like to thank the entire Amazon Web Services team for doing an amazing job providing cloud services that are revolutionizing the IT landscape. Amazon was the first to deliver on the vision of computing as a utility, and it has been a huge driver and innovator in the way we interact with compute resources. I would also like to thank the entire Apache Software Foundation CloudStack community, who works extremely hard to develop and release CloudStack—without a healthy community, there is no ecosystem (and vice versa). A huge thank you goes to Mike Tutkowski, Jeff Moody, and Pierre-Yves Ritschard, who took the time to review the book and gave me some very valuable feedback. Finally, I would like to thank Mark Hinkle, who gave me the time to write this book, and Brian Anderson, who took calls from me and brainstormed with me as we tried to figure out the best format for this book.

## PART I

Installation

This book is not about installing and configuring CloudStack (the official CloudStack documentation (*http://docs.cloudstack.apache.org*) already does a good job of that), but I feel that it is a prerequisite of this book to cover some basics about the installation process. You can certainly use this book by testing the clients and tools against a CloudStack-based public cloud and not worry about the installation. But you might also be interested in testing all of them locally, using your own deployment. In this part, we present several recipes that go through the basic source installation on both Ubuntu 14.04 and CentOS 6.5, and highlight a few interesting setups for developers—namely, the CloudStack simulator and DevCloud (the CloudStack sandbox). You will see that compiling CloudStack is quite easy: you can have a working development environment in a matter of hours. We also present a complete installation from packages for a Cloud-Stack basic zone using the KVM hypervisor. This installation will help first-time users who do not want to use the source releases.

## CHAPTER 1

Installing from Source

These recipes are aimed at CloudStack developers who need to build the code. These instructions are valid on Ubuntu 14.04 and CentOS 6.5 systems, and were tested with the 4.4 branch of Apache CloudStack; you might need to adapt them if you are on a different operating system or using a newer/older version of CloudStack. In these recipes, we cover the following items:

- Installing the prerequisites
- Compiling and installing from source
- Using the CloudStack simulator
- Testing with the CloudStack sandbox: DevCloud
- Building your own packages

 At the time of this writing, the 4.4 release is not out yet: therefore, the source testing is done on the release branch 4.4 and the packages used are the 4.3.0 packages.

1.1. Installing the Prerequisites for Ubuntu 14.04

Problem

Like any software, CloudStack has some dependencies. In this recipe, we look at installing the dependencies you'll need for Apache CloudStack development. You can use the package installation snippets to set up a machine that will allow you to build CloudStack on Ubuntu 14.04.

Solution

First, update your system. Install OpenJDK, which is our first choice, because we're using Linux. Install MySQL. Install Git to later clone the CloudStack source code. Install Maven to later build CloudStack.

Discussion

The following package installation will get the prerequisites installed on Ubuntu/Debian-based systems (this was tested on a Ubuntu 14.04 machine):

```
# apt-get -y update
# apt-get -y install openjdk-7-jdk
# apt-get -y install mysql-server
# apt-get install git
# apt-get install maven
```

MySQL should be running, but you can check its status with:

```
# service mysql status
```

This should have installed Maven 3.0.5 (you can check the version number with `mvn --version`).

A little bit of Python can be used, as we will see with the simulator described in Recipe 1.4. Therefore, install the Python package management tools:

```
# apt-get install python-pip
```

1.2. Installing the Prerequisites for CentOS 6.5

Problem

Like any software, CloudStack has some dependencies. In this recipe, we look at installing the dependencies you'll need for Apache CloudStack development. You can use the package installation snippets to set up a machine that will allow you to build CloudStack and CentOS 6.5.

Solution

First, update your system. Install OpenJDK, which is our first choice, because we're using Linux. Next, install MySQL, if it's not already present on the system. Install Git to later clone the CloudStack source code. Finally, install `mkisofs` via the `genisoimage` package.

Discussion

The following package installation snippet will get most of the prerequisites installed on a CentOS/RHEL-based system (this was tested on a CentOS 6.5 machine):

```
# yum -y update
# yum -y install java-1.7.0-openjdk
# yum -y install java-1.7.0-openjdk-devel
# yum -y install mysql-server
# yum -y install git
# yum -y install genisoimage
```

MySQL should be stopped. You can check its status with `service mysqld status` and start it with `service mysqld start`.

Let's now install Maven to build CloudStack. It is a bit more complex than on Ubuntu 14.04. Grab the 3.0.5 release from the Maven website (*http://maven.apache.org/download.cgi*):

```
# wget http://mirror.cc.columbia.edu/pub/software/apache/maven/maven-3/ \
3.0.5/binaries/apache-maven-3.0.5-bin.tar.gz
# tar xzf apache-maven-3.0.5-bin.tar.gz -C /usr/local
# cd /usr/local
# ln -s apache-maven-3.0.5 maven
```

You can set up Maven system-wide by creating a */etc/profile.d/maven.sh* file with the following content:

```
# export M2_HOME=/usr/local/maven
# export PATH=${M2_HOME}/bin:${PATH}
```

Run the following, and you will have Maven in your PATH (the preceding steps should have installed Maven 3.0; you can check the version number with `mvn --version`):

```
# source /etc/profile.d/maven.sh
# mvn --version
```

A little bit of Python can be used (see Recipe 1.4), so install the Python Package Index utility (*pip*):

```
# yum -y install python-pip
```

 CentOS 6.5 is using Python 2.6.6. To use the simulator and the CloudStack Marvin package, we will need Python 2.7 or later. Setting up Python 2.7 is left out of this recipe.

1.3. Installing from Source

Problem

With prerequisites installed (see Recipe 1.1 or Recipe 1.2), you want to build CloudStack from source and run the management server locally.

Solution

You clone the Git repository of CloudStack and use several Maven profiles to build from source, set up the database, and run the management server with Jetty (*http://www.eclipse.org/jetty/*).

Discussion

If you have gone through the prerequisite steps on Ubuntu or CentOS, then the following build steps should be identical on both systems. CloudStack uses Git for source version control; if you're not familiar with Git, the online GitHub tutorial (*http://try.github.io*) is a good start.

> The steps highlighted in this section are the minimal steps required to get a successful build of Apache CloudStack. Setting up a hypervisor, setting up storage, and running the CloudStack management server in a nondebug and production mode will require additional packages.

Once Git is set up on your machine, pull the source from the Apache repository with:

```
git clone -b 4.4 https://git-wip-us.apache.org/repos/asf/cloudstack.git
```

> The Apache CloudStack repository is also mirrored on GitHub (*http://github.com*). You might want to clone from there:
>
> ```
> git clone -b 4.4 https://github.com/apache/cloudstack.git
> ```
>
> Although I am an Apache committer, I admit that the Apache Git repo tends to be a bit slow. You will clone faster by using the GitHub mirror.

Now that you have installed the prerequisites and cloned the source code, you are ready to build the 4.4 release (which, at the time you are reading this, should be the latest stable release). To compile CloudStack, go to the CloudStack source folder and use Maven commands (if you want to skip running the unit tests, add `-DskipTests` to this command):

```
cd cloudstack
mvn -Pdeveloper,systemvm clean install
```

Next, create all the proper MySQL tables with:

```
mvn -Pdeveloper -pl developer -Ddeploydb
```

You can check what tables have been created by opening an interactive MySQL shell and looking at the *cloud* database. Runing the Apache CloudStack management server is only one command away. We'll use Jetty for testing (note that if you installed tom cat, it may be be running on port 8080, so you'll need to stop it before you use Jetty):

```
mvn -pl :cloud-client-ui jetty:run
```

This will run in the foreground and you will see the logs in stdout. To access the dashboard, open your web browser to *http://localhost:8080/client* (replace *localhost* with the IP of your management server if need be).

 If you have iptables enabled, you may have to open the ports used by CloudStack (i.e., ports 8080, 8250, and 9090). For testing, you might want to disable the firewall with ufw disable on Ubuntu or service iptables stop on CentOS, but don't forget to turn it back on if you open this machine to the public Internet.

You can now start exploring the dashboard and play with the API. Of course, we did not set up any infrastructure and there is no storage, no hypervisors, and no network defined. At this stage, you will not be able to start instances. However, you are a couple steps away from using the simulator. The next recipe shows you how to use the simulator so that you don't have to set up a physical infrastructure, which will allow you to start developing and playing with a virtual data center on your local machine.

1.4. Using the CloudStack Simulator

Problem

You want to run some functionality tests against the CloudStack management server, but you do not want to (or cannot) deploy a complete CloudStack cloud on a physical infrastructure.

Solution

Use the CloudStack simulator to set up a virtual data center. You build CloudStack with the *simulator* profile and set up some specific database tables with another Maven profile. Then you install Marvin (*http://bit.ly/Marvin_framework*), a Python-based testing framework for CloudStack. Once you start the management server again, you can use a Marvin script (*deployDataCenter.py*) to configure a simulated infrastructure.

Discussion

CloudStack comes with a simulator based on Python bindings called *Marvin*. Marvin is available in the CloudStack source code or on PyPI. With Marvin, you can simulate your data center infrastructure by providing CloudStack with a configuration file that defines the number of zones/pods/clusters/hosts, types of storage, and so on. You can then develop and test the CloudStack management server as if it were managing your production infrastructure. To use the simulator, we need to alter some of our build steps and use Marvin to configure the simulated data center.

First, do a clean build and add the `simulator` profile:

```
mvn -Pdeveloper -Dsimulator -DskipTests clean install
```

Then deploy the database and set up some simulator-specific tables and configurations using the following:

```
mvn -Pdeveloper -pl developer -Ddeploydb
mvn -Pdeveloper -pl developer -Ddeploydb-simulator
```

 As mentioned previously, the Marvin package used to configure the data center requires Python 2.7 or later, so if you are using CentOS 6.5, you will need to install it. Because it can involve building Python from source, we are not covering this step.

Next, install Marvin (note that you will need to have installed `pip` properly in the prerequisites step; the `python-dev` package is needed to install the `paramiko` module, and the `--allow-external` flag helps install the `mysql-connector-python` package):

```
sudo apt-get -y install python-dev
sudo pip install --allow-external mysql-connector-python mysql-connector-python
sudo pip install tools/marvin/dist/Marvin-0.1.0.tar.gz
```

Stop Jetty (from any previous runs) and start a new management server with a simulator profile:

```
mvn -pl :cloud-client-ui jetty:stop
mvn -pl client jetty:run -Dsimulator
```

With the management server running in the foreground, open a separate shell to set up a basic zone with Marvin:

```
python ./tools/marvin/marvin/deployDatacenter.py -i setup/dev/basic.cfg
```

At this stage, log in to the CloudStack management server at *http://localhost:8080/client* with the credentials `admin`/`password`; you should see a fully configured basic zone infrastructure. To simulate an advanced zone, replace *basic.cfg* with *advanced.cfg*. You can now start a simulated instance and take snapshots of it, in addition to running most operations that a production system would allow you to do. Using the simulator is a good way to test new features, test API clients, and run integration tests.

1.5. Using the CloudStack Sandbox: DevCloud

Problem

The simulator is not enough for your testing or demonstrations. You want to take advantage of nested virtualization to run a Xen-based hypervisor locally, and use Cloud-Stack to start virtual machines within this local hypervisor.

Solution

Use DevCloud (*http://bit.ly/_DevCloud*), a VirtualBox image, to run a Xen hypervisor on your local machine. Using Maven, you set up the database for the special DevCloud use case, and run Marvin to configure CloudStack with DevCloud. You will have a cloud with one zone, one pod, one cluster, and one host: DevCloud.

Discussion

Installing from source (see Recipe 1.3) will get you to the point of running the management server, but it does not get you any hypervisors. The simulator (see Recipe 1.4) gets you a simulated data center for testing. With DevCloud, you can run at least one hypervisor and add it to your management server the way you would a real physical machine.

DevCloud is the CloudStack sandbox. The standard version is a VirtualBox-based image, though there is also a KVM-based image for it. Here we only show steps with the VirtualBox image. For KVM, there are good instructions on the CloudStack wiki (*http://bit.ly/DevCloud-KVM*).

With DevCloud, you will run the management server on your local machine and Xen hypervisors in the DevCloud VirtualBox image. DevCloud and localhost will be connected via a host-only interface available through the VirtualBox. DevCloud also has a NAT interface to get access to the public Internet.

 You could also run the management server within DevCloud itself, avoiding the need to set up your local environment to compile Cloud-Stack from source.

DevCloud prerequisites

To get started, we need to install a few prerequisites:

1. Install VirtualBox (*http://www.virtualbox.org*) on your machine.
2. Run VirtualBox and, under Preferences, create a *host-only interface* on which you disable the DHCP server.
3. Download the DevCloud image (*http://bit.ly/DevCloud_image*).
4. In VirtualBox, under File → Import Appliance, import the DevCloud image.
5. Verify the settings under Settings, and check the "enable PAE" option in the processor menu.
6. Once the VM has booted, try to SSH to it with credentials: `root`/`password` and `ssh root@192.168.56.10`.

If successful, you can move to the machine running the management server and configure a basic zone that will have one zone, one pod, one cluster, and one hypervisor: DevCloud.

Adding DevCloud as a hypervisor

To get the management server running, we do a clean build, but when we set up the database, we use some DevCloud-specific Maven profiles that are going to fill up some tables with values that match this particular setup:

```
mvn -Pdeveloper,systemvm clean install
mvn -Pdeveloper -pl developer,tools/devcloud -Ddeploydb
```

At this stage, install Marvin like you did in Recipe 1.4:

```
pip install tools/marvin/dist/Marvin-0.1.0.tar.gz
```

Start the management server with Jetty:

```
mvn -pl client jetty:run
```

You will have a running CloudStack management server but an empty infrastructure. You are going to configure CloudStack, defining a data center with a single hypervisor. To do this, we use a Python script in the *Marvin* directory called *deployDataCenter.py*. This script takes a JSON file as input and makes the required CloudStack API calls to create the zone, pod, cluster, host, and storage components of this single hypervisor data center. Here's how to do it:

```
cd tools/devcloud
python ../marvin/marvin/deployDataCenter.py -i devcloud.cfg
```

If you are curious, check the *devcloud.cfg* file and see how the data center is defined in a JSON format.

You can now log in to the management server at *http://localhost:8080/client* and start experimenting with the UI. If the configuration went well, you should see the infrastructure defined in the Infrastructure tab in the dashboard. With the zone enabled and all components set up, you can head to the Instances tab and start an instance. The default template is a *ttylinux* template that you will be able to SSH into.

> The management server is running in your local machine, and DevCloud is used only as a hypervisor. You could potentially run the management server within DevCloud as well, or memory granted, run multiple DevClouds.

Using DevCloud is a good way to get started with CloudStack and start real instances. You can use it to learn the API and learn the CloudStack networking setup.

> As of this writing, DevCloud is broken for use with the yet to be released CloudStack 4.4. DevCloud should be fixed when 4.4 is out. There is an alternative solution being developed by a Google Summer of Code 2014 project (see Recipe 1.6).

1.6. Vagrant-Based CloudStack Testing Deployment

Problem

You like DevCloud Recipe 1.5, but you would like to use a more configurable and manageable solution based on Vagrant (Recipe 5.4) and Chef (Recipe 5.9) to start a CloudStack development environment.

Solution

Use a Vagrant-based project currently under development through the Google Summer of Code (GSoC). It will use Vagrant boxes to act as a hypervisor and as an NFS and MySQL server. You will run the CloudStack management server on your local machine and it will connect to the remote database server. You will configure the data center using Marvin, just like with DevCloud (Recipe 1.5).

Discussion

This recipe assumes that you have some knowledge of Vagrant (*http://vagrantup.com*). If not, go through Recipe 5.4 first. The configuration of the NFS and MySQL server, as well as the NAT routing, is done via Chef (*http://getchef.com*) recipes. This GSoC project aims to provide complete Chef recipes to install CloudStack.

For this recipe, you will need VirtualBox (*https://www.virtual box.org*) installed on your machine. You will also need to set up VirtualBox with a host-only (*http://bit.ly/host-only*) interface that has the DHCP server disabled.

To try this work in progress, clone what is currently called GSoC-2014 and use Vagrant to start the boxes. The project makes use of Git submodules and you will need the `--recursive` option when cloning to get the code from these subprojects:

```
git clone --recursive https://github.com/imduffy15/GSoC-2014.git
cd GSoC-2014
cd MySql_NFS_XenServer
vagrant up
```

This will start a *management* machine based on CentOS 6.5 and using Chef (Recipe 5.9). A *xenserver* machine will also be brought up to act as a hypervisor. Go back to the *cloudstack* directory, build and run the CloudStack management server on your local machine and use Marvin to configure the data center programmatically (if you need help with any of these steps, refer back to Recipe 1.3):

```
wget http://download.cloud.com.s3.amazonaws.com/tools/vhd-util \
    -P scripts/vm/hypervisor/xenserver/
chmod +x scripts/vm/hypervisor/xenserver/vhd-util
mvn -P developer,systemvm clean install -DskipTests=true
mvn -P developer -pl developer,tools/devcloud -Ddeploydb
mvn -pl :cloud-client-ui jetty:run
```

With the management server running, you can access the dashboard at *http://localhost: 8080/client*. On another shell, install Marvin and deploy the *devcloud* configuration:

```
pip install tools/marvin/dist/Marvin-0.1.0.tar.gz
python tools/marvin/marvin/deployDataCenter.py -i ../devcloud.cfg
```

To check on the status of the system VMs (Recipe 2.8), use `vagrant ssh` and once logged in on the hypervisor, use the xe toolstack to check the running VMs:

```
cd ../MySql_NFS_XenServer
vagrant ssh xenserver
sudo su
xe vm-list
```

Once the system VMs are up and running, the *ttylinux* template will get downloaded and installed and you will be able to start an instance, do all the testing that you want, and develop more CloudStack features. Enjoy!

1.7. Building CloudStack Binary Packages

Problem

Instead of using the convenience binaries available through a community-maintained repository, you want to build your own CloudStack packages from source.

Solution

Install a few more packages, which were not required for building from source. On Ubuntu, use the `dpkg-buildpackage` command, and on CentOS/RHEL systems, use the script *package.sh* located in the *packaging/centos63/* directory.

Discussion

Working from source is necessary when developing CloudStack. As mentioned earlier, this is not primarily intended for users. However, some may want to modify the code for their own use and specific infrastructure. They may also need to build their own packages for security reasons and due to network connectivity constraints. This recipe shows you the gist of how to build packages. We assume that you will know how to create a repository (*http://bit.ly/create_repo*) to serve these packages. The complete documentation is available on the website (*http://bit.ly/build_packages*).

To build Debian packages, you will need a couple extra packages that we did not need to install as prerequisites for source compilation:

```
# apt-get -y install python-mysqldb
# apt-get -y install debhelper
# apt-get -y install tomcat6
```

Then build the packages with:

```
# dpkg-buildpackage -uc -us
```

One directory up from the CloudStack root dir, you will find:

```
cloudstack_4.4.0_amd64.changes
cloudstack_4.4.0.dsc
cloudstack_4.4.0.tar.gz
cloudstack-agent_4.4.0_all.deb
cloudstack-awsapi_4.4.0_all.deb
cloudstack-cli_4.4.0_all.deb
cloudstack-common_4.4.0_all.deb
cloudstack-docs_4.4.0_all.deb
cloudstack-management_4.4.0_all.deb
cloudstack-usage_4.4.0_all.deb
```

Of course, the community provides a repository for these packages and you can use it instead of building your own packages and putting them in your own repo. Instructions on how to use this community repository are available in the installation guide (*http://bit.ly/community_repo*).

On CentOS/RHEL systems, add the following packages:

```
# yum -y install rpm-build
# yum -y install tomcat6
# yum -y install ws-commons-util
# yum -y install gcc
# yum -y install glibc-devel
# yum -y install MySQL-python
```

You can then build the packages by running *./packaging/centos63/package.sh* from the *cloudstack* directory. The rpms will be located in *./dist/rpmbuild/RPMS/x86_64*. Cloud-Stack features some plug-ins (e.g., networking, storage) that may use software with licenses that may conflict with the Apache license or that may only be made available as binaries. These plug-ins are not distributed by Apache but can be built by users with the `noredist` flag (e.g., in CentOS, use `package.sh -p noredist`).

## CHAPTER 2

Installing from Packages

Most users will not install CloudStack from source, so in this chapter, we'll look at the installation process using community-provided binaries. These instructions are valid on an Ubuntu 14.04 server system; you might need to adapt them if you are on a different operating system.

We are going to set up a CloudStack infrastructure consisting of two machines. One will be running the CloudStack management server, a MySQL database, and an NFS server. The other will be set up as a KVM hypervisor; it will mount the NFS share exported by the management server and will have a Linux bridge set up for all the virtual machines to attach to.

We will set up a *basic* networking zone (illustrated in Figure 2-1), which means that we will use a shared layer 3 network. Isolation of tenants will be through security groups; no VLANs or other layer 2 isolation method will be used. This will be very similar to the DevCloud (Recipe 1.5) setup, but will use packages instead of a source build, and KVM instead of a Xen hypervisor.

For complete installation instructions, see the official documentation (*http://bit.ly/ install_docs*); this is just a quick start guide to get you off the ground. Although the recipes can be read independently of one another, if you want to do a complete install of CloudStack, you will need to review all of the recipes in this chapter.

 The Apache Software Foundation does not release binaries, so keep in mind that these hosted packages are made available by community members for the convenience of users but do not represent official releases of the Apache CloudStack project.

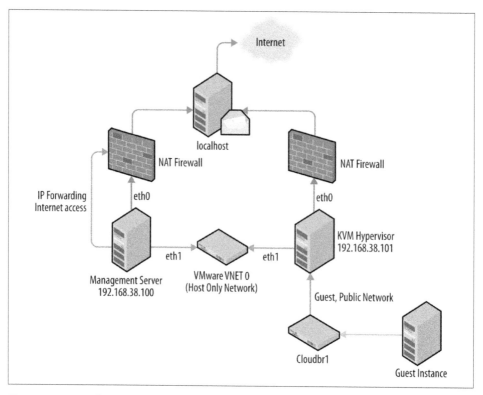

Figure 2-1. Apache CloudStack basic zone

To do this installation, we will follow five basic steps:

1. Installing the management server prerequisites
2. Setting up the management server
3. Installing the KVM agent prerequisites
4. Setting up a KVM hypervisor
5. Configuring a basic zone

2.1. Installing the Prerequisites on the Management Server

Problem

To set up the CloudStack management server on a pristine Ubuntu 14.04 server using the CloudStack community package repository, you need to install a few prerequisites and prepare your networking environment.

Solution

Use the bash command-line snippet shown in the Discussion to install the prerequisites on Ubuntu 14.04. Edit the */etc/hosts* and */etc/networking/interfaces* files to set up your network.

Discussion

Let's look at the dependencies you'll need for installing CloudStack. First, update your system, install NTP to synchronize the clocks, and install openSSH server if you have not done so already. Install a MySQL server. We will run the database and the management server on the same machine:

```
# apt-get update
# apt-get -y install openntpd
# apt-get -y install openssh-server
# apt-get -y install mysql-server
# apt-get -y install libmysql-java
```

To simplify things in this test setup, make sure that you can SSH as the root user to this server. Edit the */etc/ssh/ssh_config* file and set `PermitRootLogin` to yes. In addition, during the `mysql-server` installation, set a blank password. This is certainly not recommended for production systems, but in this simple test it will move things forward nicely.

 The need for the `libmysql-java` package is a bug in the 4.3.0 release. It is fixed in the upcoming 4.4 release and minor bug fix release 4.3.1.

Networking in cloud infrastructure can be a bit tedious, so let's try to get this right from the start. In this test infrastructure, the management server and the KVM hypervisor both have two network interfaces. One is on a public network (10.0.0.0/0) and the other one on a private network (192.18.38.0/0). The management server has IP 192.168.38.100 on the private network and the KVM hypervisor has 192.168.38.101. You can set the hostname of each server locally by editing */etc/hostname* and */etc/hosts*. On the management server, for example, you can set the following:

```
# cat /etc/hostname
server

# cat /etc/hosts
127.0.0.1        localhost
127.0.1.1        server

192.168.38.100 server server.cloud
192.168.38.101 agent agent.cloud

# The following lines are desirable for IPv6 capable hosts
::1      localhost ip6-localhost ip6-loopback
ff02::1 ip6-allnodes
ff02::2 ip6-allrouters
```

This setup allows you to ping server and agent from each machine respectively.

In terms of network interfaces, make sure that they are set up properly. Of course, your personal setup may vary. In this recipe, the eth0 interface gets an IP from a DHCP server and provides the route to the public Internet. The eth1 interface is assigned an IP address statically. This results in the following *route* and */etc/network/interfaces* file:

```
# cat /etc/network/interfaces
# This file describes the network interfaces available on your system
# and how to activate them. For more information, see interfaces(5).

# The loopback network interface
auto lo
iface lo inet loopback

# The primary network interface
auto eth0
iface eth0 inet dhcp
    dns_nameservers 8.8.8.8 8.8.4.4
    post-up route add default gw 10.0.0.1

auto eth1
iface eth1 inet static
    address 192.168.38.100
    gateway 192.168.38.1
    netmask 255.255.255.0

root@server:/home/sebgoa# route
Kernel IP routing table
Destination     Gateway       Genmask         Flags Metric Ref    Use Iface
default         10.0.0.1      0.0.0.0         UG    0      0        0 eth0
10.0.0.0        *             255.255.255.0   U     0      0        0 eth0
192.168.38.0    *             255.255.255.0   U     0      0        0 eth1
root@server:/home/sebgoa#
```

Make sure that you can reach the public Internet and that you can ping your private gateway. If you are jumping ahead and setting up the agent at the same time, make sure you can ping the agent on its private address.

This is all you need to start on a solid foundation and run the management server.

2.2. Setting Up the Management Server

Problem

With the prerequisites met (see Recipe 2.1), you want to configure the CloudStack community package repository and get the packages to run the management server. Then you want to set up the database and start the management server.

Solution

Add the CloudStack repo to the list of repositories that your system can get packages from and set up the database tables using the `cloudstack-setup-databases` script that will be in your path. Set up the management server with `cloudstack-setup-management` and launch the service with `service cloudstack-management start`.

Discussion

As mentioned, packages are being hosted in a community repo. To get the packages, add the CloudStack repo to your list by editing */etc/apt/sources.list.d/cloudstack.list* and adding the following:

```
deb http://cloudstack.apt-get.eu/ubuntu precise 4.3
```

Replace 4.3 with the release number that you want. At the time of this writing, the 4.4 release is not out, so you should still use 4.3 until 4.4 comes out. Add the public keys to the trusted keys and update your local apt cache:

```
wget -O - http://cloudstack.apt-get.eu/release.asc|apt-key add -
apt-get update
```

 You will need to set up the same package repository on your KVM hypervisor (see Recipe 2.4).

With the repository set up, you can now grab the management server packages:

```
apt-get install cloudstack-management
```

This will install several dependencies. Once this is complete, you are ready to set up the database. CloudStack can make use of a database running on a separate node, but in this quick start guide, we are setting up everything on the same machine. Go ahead and configure the database with the following command:

```
cloudstack-setup-databases cloud:<dbpassword>@localhost \
--deploy-as=root:<password> \
-e <encryption_type> \
-m <management_server_key> \
-k <database_key> \
-i <management_server_ip>
```

If you deploy as *root* with no password (as was recommended earlier) and don't use encryption, the output of running this setup command should be something similar to the following:

```
# cloudstack-setup-databases cloud:cloud@localhost --deploy-as=root
Mysql user name:cloud                                                      [ OK ]
Mysql user password:******                                                 [ OK ]
Mysql server ip:localhost                                                  [ OK ]
Mysql server port:3306                                                     [ OK ]
Mysql root user name:root                                                  [ OK ]
Mysql root user password:******                                            [ OK ]
Checking Cloud database files ...                                          [ OK ]
Checking local machine hostname ...                                        [ OK ]
Checking SELinux setup ...                                                 [ OK ]
Detected local IP address as 185.19.28.99,
will use as cluster management server node IP[ OK ]
Preparing /etc/cloudstack/management/db.properties                         [ OK ]
Applying /usr/share/cloudstack-management/setup/create-database.sql        [ OK ]
Applying /usr/share/cloudstack-management/setup/create-schema.sql          [ OK ]
Applying /usr/share/cloudstack-management/setup/create-database-premium.sql[ OK ]
Applying /usr/share/cloudstack-management/setup/create-schema-premium.sql  [ OK ]
Applying /usr/share/cloudstack-management/setup/server-setup.sql           [ OK ]
Applying /usr/share/cloudstack-management/setup/templates.sql              [ OK ]
Processing encryption ...                                                  [ OK ]
Finalizing setup ...                                                       [ OK ]

CloudStack has successfully initialized database, you can check your database
configuration in /etc/cloudstack/management/db.properties
```

You are now ready to finish the setup and start the management server. The following command will set up iptables properly, provide sudoers access, and restart the management server:

```
cloudstack-setup-management
```

You can check the status or restart the management server with the following:

```
service cloudstack-management <status|restart>
```

You should now be able to log in to the management server UI at *http://localhost:8080/client* (replace *localhost* with the appropriate IP address if needed). The default login is *admin* and the default password is *password*. Click on the "I have used Cloud-Stack before" icon and go straight to the main dashboard. At this stage, you have the CloudStack management server running, but no hypervisors and no storage configured.

2.3. Setting Up an Image Catalog and Seeding it with the SystemVM Template

Problem

You need to build an image catalog accessible by all the hypervisors in your cloud. You also need to seed this image catalog with the template of the CloudStack system virtual machines (SVM). These SVMs run in the cloud itself and are used by CloudStack to orchestrate certain functionalities like snapshots, console proxy, and network services.

Solution

Set up an NFS server and export the NFS share to your hypervisor. Use a CloudStack script installed during the management server setup to fetch the template of the SVM and store it in the NFS share.

Discussion

CloudStack has two types of storage: primary and secondary. The *primary* storage is defined at the cluster level and available on the hypervisors that make up a cluster. In this installation, we will use local storage for primary storage. The secondary storage is shared zone wide and hosts the image templates and snapshots. In this installation, we will use a NFS server running on the same node that we used to run the management server.

Install NFS packages:

```
apt-get install nfs-kernel-server portmap
mkdir -p /export/secondary
chown nobody:nogroup /export/secondary
```

The hypervisors in your infrastructure as well as the secondary storage VM will mount this secondary storage. Edit */etc/exports* in such a way that these nodes can mount the share. For instance:

```
/export/secondary 192.168.38.0/24(rw,async,fsid=0,no_root_squash)
```

Then create the NFS table for your export and start the NFS server service:

```
exportfs -a
service nfs-kernel-server start
```

We are not setting up any firewall rules at this time for the NFS server.

We now need to seed this secondary storage with *SystemVM* templates. SystemVMs are small appliances that run on one of the hypervisors of your infrastructure and help orchestrate the cloud. We have the *secondary storage VM*, which manages image placement and snapshots; the *proxy VM*, which handles VNC connections to the instances; and the *virtual router*, which provides network services. To seed the secondary storage with the system VM template on Ubuntu for a KVM hypervisor:

```
# /usr/share/cloudstack-common/scripts/storage/secondary/cloud-install-sys-tmplt \
-m /export/secondary \
-u http://download.cloud.com/templates/4.3 \
/systemvm64template-2014-01-14-master-kvm.qcow2.bz2 \
-h kvm -s <optional-management-server-secret-key> -F \
```

In this setup, we don't use a management server secret key, so you don't need to specify an -s option.

2.4. Preparing a KVM Hypervisor

Problem

You have the management server running, but you still need to set up a hypervisor. CloudStack is hypervisor agnostic and therefore suppports VMware Esxi, Hyper-V, XenServer, LXC, and KVM. To set up a KVM hypervisor with CloudStack, you need to mount the secondary storage and install the CloudStack agent on it.

Solution

On a fresh Ubuntu 14.04 server, install the NFS client and mount the secondary storage that you set up in Recipe 2.3. After having set up the CloudStack package repository (Recipe 2.2), you install the KVM CloudStack agent and finally set the hostname and local DNS names properly.

Discussion

In this recipe, we will set up an Ubuntu 14.04 KVM hypervisor. The Secondary storage set up in Recipe 2.3 needs to be mounted on this node. Let's start by making this mount.

First, install openntpd (a service for time synchronization) on this server as well as the NFS client packages. Then mount the secondary storage NFS filesystem exported from the management server:

```
apt-get install openntpd
apt-get install nfs-common portmap
mkdir -p /mnt/export/secondary
mount -t nfs 192.168.38.100:/export/secondary /mnt/export/secondary
```

Check that the mount is successful with the df -h or the mount command. Then create a file in the mounted directory by running touch /mnt/export/secondary/foobar. Verify that you can also edit the file from the management server.

To make sure that this mount is made after a reboot, edit *etc/fstab* and add this line:

```
192.168.38.100:/export/secondary /mnt/export/secondary nfs auto 0 0
```

 For primary storage, we will use local storage. This will be set up when we configure the infrastructure. You will need to set the configuration variable systemvm.use.local.storage to True and restart the management server.

Similar to what you did with the management server, set the hostname and the local DNS names of the agent. Edit the *etc/hostname* and *etc/hosts/* files to be:

```
# cat /etc/hostname
agent

# cat /etc/hosts
127.0.0.1       localhost
127.0.1.1       agent

192.168.38.100 server server.cloud
192.168.38.101 agent agent.cloud

# The following lines are desirable for IPv6 capable hosts
::1     localhost ip6-localhost ip6-loopback
ff02::1 ip6-allnodes
ff02::2 ip6-allrouters
```

Interaction between the management server and the KVM hypervisor happens through an agent running on the hypervisor. This agent is written in Java and makes use of libvirt-java bindings to manage instances started on the host. To install the agent, add the CloudStack repository the same way that you did when installing the management server (see Recipe 2.2):

```
echo deb http://cloudstack.apt-get.eu/ubuntu precise 4.3 \
    > /etc/apt/sources.list.d/cloudstack.list
wget -O - http://cloudstack.apt-get.eu/release.asc|apt-key add -
apt-get update
```

You can then install the CloudStack KVM agent with:

```
apt-get -y install cloudstack-agent
```

But don't start the agent yet; let's configure libvirt first.

2.5. Configuring libvirt

Problem

The CloudStack agent for KVM uses the *libvirt* Java bindings. You need to configure libvirt properly for the CloudStack KVM agent to work.

Solution

Edit */etc/libvirt/libvirt.conf* and */etc/init/libvirt-bin.conf* to set a few variables and establish your security policies. If apparmor is running, disable the security policies for libvirt; if it's not running, then you are set.

Discussion

libvirt (*http://libvirt.org*) is a common API for most hypervisor technologies used to create virtual machines within physical servers. You will see that libvirt is a dependency of the CloudStack agent package on KVM hypervisor. Once the agent is installed, you need to configure libvirt.

Edit */etc/libvirt/libvirt.conf* to include:

```
listen_tls = 0
listen_tcp = 1
tcp_port = "16509"
auth_tcp = "none"
mdns_adv = 0
```

In addition, edit */etc/init/libvirt-bin.conf* to modify the libvirt options like so:

```
env libvirtd_opts="-d -l"
```

Then restart libvirt:

```
service libvirt-bin restart
```

To check whether security policies are configured properly, check that apparmor is running with dpkg --list 'apparmor'. If it's not, then you have nothing to do. If it is, then enter the following commands:

```
ln -s /etc/apparmor.d/usr.sbin.libvirtd /etc/apparmor.d/disable/
ln -s /etc/apparmor.d/usr.lib.libvirt.virt-aa-helper /etc/apparmor.d/disable/
apparmor_parser -R /etc/apparmor.d/usr.sbin.libvirtd
apparmor_parser -R /etc/apparmor.d/usr.lib.libvirt.virt-aa-helper
```

2.6. Basic Zone Network Configuration and NAT Router Setup

Problem

You have installed the CloudStack packages and set up your secondary storage. lib virt is configured properly and you have set up the hostnames and local DNS names. The missing step is to configure the network to give network connectivity to the virtual machines that you will provision through CloudStack. In this setup, we assume a basic zone where all virtual machines share the same layer 2 network. A CloudStack advanced zone would isolate all users on different layer 2 networks using a network isolation method (e.g., VLANs). In addition, we will carry all the management, guest, storage, and public traffic through the same physical network. CloudStack could use multiple physical networks to carry the traffic of each of these, but we are not doing it in this recipe. Hence, the problem is to set up a virtual switch on the KVM hypervisor so that virtual interfaces can be connected to this switch and traffic can be forwarded properly. Specifically, we need to carry the public Internet traffic through the management server public Internet address.

Solution

You need to configure the network so that the KVM agent has a Linux bridge (virtual switch) set up, where the virtual machines will attach to. You also need to set up IP forwarding on the management server to provide public Internet access from the private network. Edit the */etc/network/interfaces* on the KVM agent to add one Linux bridge. Turn on IPv4 forwarding on the management server and configure a few iptables rules to route traffic from the private network interface to the public network interface.

Discussion

Let's start by setting up IPv4 forwarding on the management server:

```
# sysctl net.ipv4.ip_forward
net.ipv4.ip_forward = 0
# sysctl -w net.ipv4.ip_forward=1
net.ipv4.ip_forward = 1
# sysctl net.ipv4.ip_forward
net.ipv4.ip_forward = 1
```

Edit */etc/sysctl.conf* to set it up after reboot (uncomment the net.ipv4.ip_forward=1 line).

Set up iptables forwarding and save the rules:

```
# iptables -t nat -A POSTROUTING -o eth0 -j MASQUERADE
# iptables -A FORWARD -i eth1 -o eth0 -j ACCEPT
```

```
# iptables -A FORWARD -i eth0 -o eth1 -m state \
        --state RELATED,ESTABLISHED -j ACCEPT
# iptables-save > /etc/iptables.rules
```

We are now going to set up the network bridge on the KVM hypervisor. It is used to give network connectivity to the instances that will run on this hypervisor. This configuration can change depending on the number of network interfaces you have or whether you use VLANS or not. In our simple case, we only have one network interface on the hypervisor and no VLANs.

 We originally set up two network interfaces on the KVM hypervisor. This made it easy to get public Internet access when setting up the machine. However, from a CloudStack standpoint, we will only use the private network interface. Hence, CloudStack will only see one physical network and only requires one Linux bridge on the hypervisor. You could set things up with multiple physical networks: in this situation, you would set up multiple bridges and use KVM traffic labels to differentiate them within CloudStack.

You configure the bridge by editing the */etc/network/interfaces* file like so:

```
# cat /etc/network/interfaces
# This file describes the network interfaces available on your system
# and how to activate them. For more information, see interfaces(5).

# The loopback network interface
auto lo
iface lo inet loopback

# The primary network interface
auto eth0
iface eth0 inet dhcp

# The secondary network interface
auto eth1
iface eth1 inet manual

#Private bridge
auto cloudbr1
iface cloudbr1 inet static
    address 192.168.38.101
    dns_nameservers 8.8.8.8 8.8.4.4
    netmask 255.255.255.0
    gateway 192.168.38.100
    bridge_ports eth1
    bridge_fd 5
    bridge_stp off
    bridge_maxwait 1
```

Note that the gateway on `cloudbr1` is set to be the server. Reboot the agent to take these changes into account. After the reboot, check that the routes are set properly and that you can ping the server and reach the public Internet:

```
# route
Kernel IP routing table
Destination     Gateway         Genmask         Flags Metric Ref    Use Iface
default         server          0.0.0.0         UG    0      0        0 cloudbr1
10.0.0.0        *               255.255.255.0   U     0      0        0 eth0
192.168.38.0    *               255.255.255.0   U     0      0        0 cloudbr1
192.168.122.0   *               255.255.255.0   U     0      0        0 virbr0
```

The final step is to start the CloudStack agent:

```
service cloudstack-agent start
```

2.7. Configuring a Basic Zone

Problem

You have set up your management server and KVM hypervisor, your image catalog is ready to go, and your network is all set. Now is the time to configure your CloudStack cloud through the management dashboard. We will be configuring a basic zone, which means that we will be configuring the nodes, storage servers, IP addresses, etc. that CloudStack will need to be aware of to orchestrate virtual machine provisioning in this infrastructure.

Solution

Go through the dashboard, select the Infrastructure tab, click on the Zone icon and select Add Zone. Then follow the wizard. Once the zone is enabled, and all components are green and the system VMs are running, you are ready to start an instance.

Discussion

You have set up the management server (Recipe 2.2), created a secondary storage for an image catalog (Recipe 2.3), set up a KVM hypervisor (Recipe 2.4), and configured the network for a basic zone deployment (Recipe 2.6). You are now ready to go through the dashboard and configure your cloud.

CloudStack, like AWS EC2, has the concept of availability zones. To get started, you will create a zone and follow the dashboard wizard. This wizard will guide you through creating a pod, a cluster, and a host, as well as defining your primary and secondary storage. For more information on this terminology, check the online documentation (*http://docs.cloudstack.apache.org/en/master/concepts.html*).

Log in to the management server UI *http://192.168.38.100:8080/client*. Replace the IP with the IP of your management server. Log in with the username *admin* and the password *password*. You can be adventurous and click where you want or keep on following this recipe. Click the button that says "I have used CloudStack before, skip this guide"; we are going to bypass the wizard. You will then see the admin view of the dashboard. Click the Infrastructure tab on the left side. Click the View Zones icon and find and follow the Add Zone icon on the top right. You will then follow a series of windows where you have to enter information describing the zone.

Our zone is a basic zone with 8.8.8.8 as primary DNS and 8.8.4.4 as internal DNS. Our hypervisor type is KVM, and we are using local storage (scroll drown to the bottom of the wizard window).

The reserved IPs are IPs used by the system VMs. Allocate a slice of your private network to this (e.g., 192.168.38.10 to 192.168.38.20) and specify the gateway and netmask (192.168.38.100 and 255.255.255.0).

The guest network will be another slice of this private network (e.g., 192.168.38.150 to 192.168.38.200 with gateway 192.168.38.100 and netmask 255.255.255.0).

The host is the KVM hypervisor that we set up. Enter its IP: 192.168.38.101 and its root password. Make sure that you can SSH as root to the host with that password.

Finally, add the secondary storage. In our case, it is the NFS server we set up on the management server (i.e., 192.168.38.100 and with a path of */export/secondary*).

Once you are done entering the information, launch the zone, and CloudStack will configure everything. If everything goes well, all the steps should have turned green. We are using local storage on the hypervisor, so we will need to go to the Global Setttings tab and set that up. We saw a warning during the configuration phase to that effect. In the search icon (top right), enter `system`; you should see the setting `system.vm.use.lo cal.storage`. Set it to true and restart the management server `service cloudstack-management restart`. At this stage, CloudStack will start by trying to run the system VMs and you should see a dashboard similar to the one shown in Figure 2-2.

You may face your first troubleshooting issue (Recipe 2.8), especially if your hypervisor does not have much RAM. You can define some overprovisioning factor to overcome this issue. In Global Settings, look up the `mem.overprovisioning.factor` variable and set it to something larger than 1. You can do the same thing with CPU overprovisioning with the `cpu.overprovisioning.factor`. You will be prompted to restart the management server.

If all goes well, the system VMs will start, and you should be able to start adding templates and launch instances. On KVM, your templates will need to be qcow2 images with a *qcow2* file extension. You will also need to have this image on a web server that is reachable by your management server. However, to test your configuration, you will see that there is a default CentOS 5.5 template already present. When the secondary system VM started, this template should have started to download; when it reaches Ready state, you can use it.

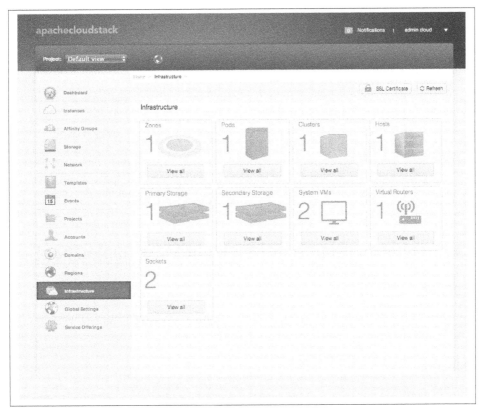

Figure 2-2. Apache CloudStack dashboard

The last step is to define a *compute offering* that matches your cloud. By default, a CloudStack installation will have two compute offerings: small and medium instance. Both assume shared storage for primary storage. This means that they will not work with our setup where we are using local storage. Hence, you need to create a new compute offering with *local storage* enabled. Click in the Service Offerings tab, and in the "select offering" drop-down menu, select Compute Offerings. Then click the Add Compute Offering button, fill in the information in the form, and add it.

If you use the `DefaultShareNetworkwithSecurityGroup` network of-fering when creating your zone (which is the default), don't forget to add ingress rules to that default security group, otherwise, no in-bound traffic will be allowed to your instances. To ping your instances, allow `ICMP Echo request (type=8, code=0)`.

Once your systemVMs are up and you have a template (or ISO) available, you are ready to launch an instance. Go to the Instances tab and walk through the dialog screens.

Congratulations! You just completed your first CloudStack installation from scratch.

 There are configuration management recipes to ease this setup. Check out these Chef recipes (*https://github.com/cloudops/cookbook_co-cloudstack*). There are also Ansible playbooks (*http://shapeblue.com/cloudstack/deploying-cloudstack-with-ansible/*) and Puppet mani-fests (*https://github.com/CloudStack-extras/puppet-cloudstack*), even though these last ones need a bit of love.

2.8. Troubleshooting Your First CloudStack Deployment

Problem

You have created and launched a zone, and everything seems green, but your systemVMs are not starting or your templates do not get downloaded.

Solution

If the systemVMs don't start, make sure that there is enough RAM and CPU available on your hypervisor. You can turn on overprovisioning if you cannot add RAM. If your templates do not get downloaded but your secondary system VM is up, log in to it and run the system VM check.

Discussion

Following the previous recipes should get you to a working setup. However, depending on what type of hardware you used for your hypervisor, you may not have enough capacity to start the virtual machines. By default, the console proxy VMs will use 1 GB of RAM and the secondary storage VM will use 512 MB. There are several ways to deal with this:

- Add another hypervisor (follow Recipe 2.4 and add the new hypervisor through the dashboard).
- Set some overprovisioning factors under Global Settings to greater than 1.

- Change the RAM usage of the systemVMs in the database and restart the management server.

To set the overprovisioning factors, in Global Settings, look up the `mem.overprovisioning.factor` variable and set it to something larger than 1. You can do the same thing with CPU overprovisioning with the `cpu.overprovisioning.factor`. You will be prompted to restart the management server.

To change the RAM usage of the systemVMs, log in on the management server, launch a MySQL shell, and update the `service_offering` table. Check the `id` of the secondary storage and console proxy VMs:

```
mysql -u root
mysql> use cloud;
mysql> select * from service_offering;
mysql> update service_offering set ram_size=256 where id=9;
```

If your templates do not get downloaded or seem *stuck*, log in to the secondary storage system VMs from the hypervisor that is running it using the link local address of the VM (you get it from the dashboard). Then run the system check script:

```
ssh -i /root/.ssh/id_rsa.cloud -p 3922 root@169.254.x.x
/usr/local/cloud/systemvm/ssvm-check.sh
```

The *ssvm-check.sh* script will verify that it can reach various nodes in the network and that the secondary storage is accessible. If the check fails, you will need to go through your network setup again and make sure that your secondary storage is properly mounted on the hypervisor and on the secondary storage VM. There is additional detailed information on the wiki (*http://bit.ly/CloudStack_wiki*).

These few things seem to be the biggest causes of heartache when installing CloudStack, but these guidelines should help you overcome any issues!

## PART II

Clients and API Wrappers

Now that you have access to a working CloudStack setup, it is time to dive into using the API that it provides. Clients are software that run on your machine to connect to the cloud and provide easy-to-use programming methods to make API calls to the cloud endpoint you are using. There are over 20 clients for CloudStack currently available on GitHub. You should be able to find one in the programming language of your choice.

In this part, we introduce the method used to sign API requests and then present a few clients (see Figure II-1) that are commonly used by CloudStack operators and users. CloudMonkey and Apache Libcloud are Python modules, jclouds is in Java, CloStack is for Clojure, and StackerBee is for Ruby. There are many more.

All functionalities of CloudStack are exposed via an API server. There are currently over 20 clients for this API on GitHub (*http://bit.ly/GitHub_clients*), in various languages. In this part, we introduce this API and the signing mechanism. The recipes in Chapter 3 will introduce clients that already contain a signing method. The signing process is only highlighted for completeness; all clients implement it. The recipes in Chapter 4 will introduce API wrappers that provide a mapping between the CloudStack API and the APIs defined by public clouds or standard organizations.

The CloudStack API is a query-based API using HTTP, which returns results in XML or JSON. It is not a REST API in the strict definition, because it only uses HTTP verbs GET and POST. DELETE, PATCH, and UPDATE, for example, are not used. The format of the request also does not use a nice URI design like in the Google Compute Engine API (*http://bit.ly/GCE_API*). It is a query-based API similar to the EC2 query API (*http://bit.ly/query_API*).

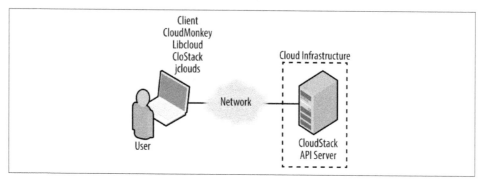

Figure II-1. Apache CloudStack clients

While clients are by definition client-side software, there is another way to abstract the CloudStack API—for example, by offering API servers that provide the well-known Amazon web services API, or the Google Compute Engine (GCE) API or even a standard API like OCCI from the Open Grid Forum (OGF). These servers (see Figure II-2) run on your machine or on the cloud provider's servers and provide a new endpoint to a CloudStack cloud. This new endpoint exposes different APIs and forwards the requests to CloudStack by mapping the inbound API call to the appropriate Cloud-Stack API. Using these API interfaces is very handy if you are already accustomed to the tools (e.g., command line, libraries) of public clouds like AWS and GCE and want to keep on using the same tooling with your private CloudStack cloud. It's also useful if you want to provide some hybrid cloud functionality between AWS/GCE and a public cloud running CloudStack.

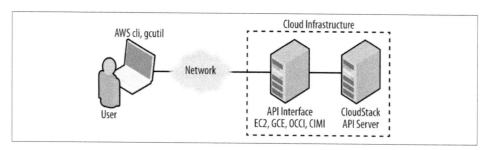

Figure II-2. Apache CloudStack interfaces

## CHAPTER 3

API Clients

3.1. The CloudStack API

The CloudStack API is not a standard like OGF OCCI (*http://occi-wg.org*) or DMTF CIMI (*http://dmtf.org/standards/cloud*), but is easy to learn. A mapping exists between the AWS API and the CloudStack API, as we will see in Chapter 4. Recently, a Google Compute Engine interface was also developed that maps the GCE REST API to the CloudStack API described here. The API docs (*http://cloudstack.apache.org/docs/ api/*) are a good place to start learning the extent of the API. Multiple clients exist on GitHub (*http://bit.ly/GitHub_clients*) to use this API, and you should be able to find one in your favorite language. The reference documentation for the API and changes that might occur from version to version is available online (*http://docs.cloud stack.apache.org/projects/cloudstack-release-notes*). This short section is aimed at providing a quick summary to give you a base understanding of how to use this API. As a quick start, a good way to explore the API is to navigate the dashboard with a firebug console (or similar developer console) to study the queries.

In a succinct statement, the CloudStack query API can be used via HTTP GET requests made against your cloud endpoint (e.g., *http://localhost:8080/client/api*). The API name is passed using the `command` key, and the various parameters for this API call are passed as key/value pairs. The request is signed using the secret key of the user making the call. Some calls are synchronous; while some are asynchronous, this is documented in the API docs (*http://cloudstack.apache.org/docs/api/*). Asynchronous calls return a `jobid`, and the status and result of a job can be queried with the `queryAsyncJobResult` call. Let's get started and give an example of calling the `listUsers` API in Python.

For more on CloudStack RESTful versus REST-like characteristics, you might be interested to read a blog post of mine: To REST or not to REST (*http://bit.ly/REST_or_not*).

Problem

To interact with your cloud programmatically, you need a set of API keys. Every cloud has the same concept, which allows you to sign API requests. You have two keys: an access key and a secret key.

Solution

In CloudStack, you generate your keys on the default dashboard within the Accounts and Users panel. If you are using a public cloud based on CloudStack, they may give you your keys at signup or through their own dashboard. Once you have your API keys, you can form the API request as an HTTP GET request with a signature. The signature is computed using Hashed Message Authentication Code (HMAC) (*http://bit.ly/comput ing_signature*) and some `base64` and `url` encoding.

Discussion

First, let's get your keys. If you have access to the default dashboard of CloudStack, go under Accounts, select the appropriate account, and then click Show Users. Select the intended user and generate keys using the Generate Keys icon. You will see an API Key and Secret Key field being generated. The keys will be of the form:

```
API Key : XzAz0uC0t888gOzPs3HchY72qwDc7pUPIO8LxC
         -VkIHo4C3fvbEBY_Ccj8fo3mBapN5qRDg_0_EbGdbxi8oy1A
Secret Key: zmBOXAXPlfb-LIygOxUVblAbz7E47eukDS_0
           JYUxP3JAmknOYo56T0R-AcM7rK7SMyo11Y6XW22gyuXzOdiybQ
```

Getting your API keys is crucial if you want to use any of the tools described in the book.

There is an API call `registerUserKeys` (*http://bit.ly/registerUser Keys*) that can be used to get the keys programmatically. However, this call is only allowed on the unsecure integration port and is only allowed for administrators of the cloud.

3.2. Signing an API Request

Problem

Now that you have your API keys, you want to form an API request and sign it.

Solution

An API request is an HTTP GET request made to the cloud endpoint. The request uses a query syntax similar to the AWS EC2 requests (*http://bit.ly/query_API*). A command key specifies the name of the API call, a set of parameters are passed as key/value pairs separated by an ampersand, and a signature built with HMAC is added.

Discussion

Let's do a step-by-step walkthrough of creating a request. Open a Python shell and import the basic modules necessary to make the request. Note that this request could be made many different ways, and this is just a low-level example. The urllib* modules are used to make the HTTP request and perform URL encoding. The hashlib module gives us the sha1 hash function. It is used to generate the hmac (Keyed Hashing for Message Authentication) using the secretkey. The result is encoded using the base64 module:

```
$python
Python 2.7.3 (default, Nov 17 2012, 19:54:34)
[GCC 4.2.1 Compatible Apple Clang 4.1 ((tags/Apple/clang-421.11.66))] on darwin
Type "help", "copyright", "credits" or "license" for more information.
>>> import urllib2
>>> import urllib
>>> import hashlib
>>> import hmac
>>> import base64
```

Define the endpoint of the cloud, the command that you want to execute, the type of the response (i.e., XML or JSON), and the keys of the user. Note that we do not put the secretkey in our request dictionary, because it is only used to compute the hmac:

```
>>> baseurl='http://localhost:8080/client/api?'
>>> request={}
>>> request['command']='listUsers'
>>> request['response']='json'
>>> request['apikey']='plgWJfZK4gyS3mOMTVmjUVg-X-jlWlnfaUJ9 \
...GAbBbf9EdM-kAYMmAiLqzzq1ElZLYq_u38zCm0bewzGUdP66mg'
>>> secretkey='VDaACYb0LV9eNjTetIOElcVQkvJck_J_QljX_FcHRj87 \
...ZKiy0z0ty0ZsYBkoXkY9b7EhwJaw7FF3akA3KBQ'
```

Of course, replace the baseurl with the endpoint that you have access to and replace the apikey and secretkey with your own.

Build the base request string, the combination of all the key/value pairs of the request. In this example, we use the Python `join` function and we iterate over all the keys of the request with `request.keys()`. Make sure to URL encode each value. Finally, join everything with an ampersand:

```
>>> request_str='&'.join(['='.join([k,urllib.quote_plus(request[k])])
                for k in request.keys()])
>>> request_str
'apikey=plgWJfZK4gyS3mOMTVmjUVg-X-jlWlnfaUJ9GAbBbf9EdM \
...-kAYMmAiLqzzq1ElZLYq_u38zCm0bewzGUdP66mg&command=listUsers&response=json'
```

Now we need to compute the signature. The signature is based on the `hmac` of the signature string with the `secretkey` using the `sha1` hash function. The resultant `hmac` is subsequently 64-bit encoded and URL encoded.

The signature string used is similar to the base request string just shown, but the keys/ values are lowercase and joined in a sorted order. The + signs are also replaced with %20:

```
>>> sig_str='&'.join(['='.join([k.lower(),urllib.quote_plus(request[k] \
....lower().replace('+','%20'))])for k in sorted(request.iterkeys())])
>>> sig_str
'apikey=plgwjfzk4gys3momtvmjuvg-x-jlwlnfauj9gabbbf9edm-kaymmailqzzq \
...1elzlyq_u38zcm0bewzgudp66mg&command=listusers&response=json'
>>> sig=hmac.new(secretkey,sig_str,hashlib.sha1).digest()
>>> sig
'M:]\x0e\xaf\xfb\x8f\xf2y\xf1p\x91\x1e\x89\x8a\xa1\x05\xc4A\xdb'
>>> sig=base64.encodestring(hmac.new(secretkey,sig_str,hashlib.sha1).digest())
>>> sig
'TTpdDq/7j/J58XCRHomKoQXEQds=\n'
>>> sig=urllib.quote_plus(base64.encodestring(hmac.new( \
...secretkey,sig_str,hashlib.sha1).digest()).strip())
```

Finally, build the entire API request string by joining the `baseurl`, the request string, and the signature. You just need to use HTTP GET to get the response (HTTP POST is also supported for some API calls). In Python, we can just add everything up and use `urllib2.urlopen()`:

```
>>> req=baseurl+request_str+'&signature='+sig
>>> req
'http://localhost:8080/client/api?apikey=plgWJfZK4gyS3mOMTVmjUVg ↵

 -X-jlWlnfaUJ9GAbBbf9EdM-kAYMmAiLqzzq1ElZLYq_u38zCm0bewzGUdP66mg ↵

&command=listUsers&response=json&signature=TTpdDq%2F7j%2FJ58XCRHomKoQXEQds%3D'
>>> res=urllib2.urlopen(req)
>>> res.read()
'{ "listusersresponse" : { "count":1 ,"user" :
  [ {"id":"7ed6d5da-93b2-4545-a502-23d20b48ef2a",
     "username":"admin","firstname":"admin",
     "lastname":"cloud","created":"2012-07-05T12:18:27-0700",
```

```
        "state":"enabled","account":"admin",
    "accounttype":1,"domainid":"8a111e58-e155-4482-93ce-84efff3c7c77",
        "domain":"ROOT",
    "apikey":"plgWJfZK4gyS3mOMTVmjUVg-X-jlWlnfaUJ9GAbBbf9EdM ↵

                -kAYMmAiLqzzq1ElZLYq_u38zCm0bewzGUdP66mg",
    "secretkey":"VDaACYb0LV9eNjTetIOElcVQkvJck_J_QljX_FcHRj8
                7ZKiy0z0ty0ZshwJaw7FF3akA3KBQ",
    "accountid":"7548ac03-af1d-4c1c-9064-2f3e2c0eda0d"}]}}
```

All the clients that you will find on GitHub will implement this signature technique, so you should not have to do it by hand. However, it's a great exercise to get familiar with the API and understand how you can make requests to a cloud programmatically.

3.3. Installing CloudMonkey, the CloudStack Interactive Shell

CloudMonkey is a subproject of Apache CloudStack and gives operators/developers the ability to use any of the API methods. As of CloudStack 4.2, it has nice autocompletion, history, and help features as well as an API discovery mechanism.

CloudMonkey can be used both as an interactive shell and as a command-line tool that simplifies CloudStack configuration and management. It can be used with CloudStack 4.0-incubating release and later.

 CloudMonkey is terrific because it gives you 100% coverage of the CloudStack API. However, because you are using every call directly, it can be a bit overwhelming, and some commands may appear a bit lengthy.

Problem

You want use an interactive shell to configure, administer, or use your CloudStack cloud. You are also looking for a CloudStack client that has 100% API coverage with which you can write shell scripts.

Solution

Install CloudMonkey from a community-maintained package distribution or from source using the Apache repository.

Discussion

CloudMonkey is dependent on readline, pygments, and prettytable. When installing from source, you will need to resolve those dependencies. Using the PyPI repository, the dependencies will be automatically installed.

There are two ways to get CloudMonkey: via the official CloudStack source releases or via a community-maintained distribution in PyPI (*http://bit.ly/CloudMonkey*).

Users will want to use the community-maintained package on PyPI (*http://bit.ly/_CloudMonkey*), and will install CloudMonkey in a single command:

```
$ sudo pip install cloudmonkey
```

Developers who want to look at the code should use the official Apache CloudStack CloudMonkey Git repository, clone the repository, and install it:

```
$ git clone https://git-wip-us.apache.org/repos/asf/cloudstack-cloudmonkey.git
$ sudo python setup.py install
```

If the installation is successful, you should be able to open the *cloudmonkey_ interactive* shell by typing cloudmonkey in the command line. The following output should appear:

```
$ cloudmonkey
☁ Apache CloudStack cloudmonkey 5.0.0. Type help or ? to list commands.

>
```

You can use CloudMonkey as an interactive shell, but it can be used as a straightfoward CLI, passing the commands to the cloudmonkey command as shown here:

```
$ cloudmonkey list users
```

As such, it can be used in shell scripts, it can receive commands via stdin, and its output can be parsed like any other Unix commands via grep or awk or whichever command you need to use to process it.

3.4. Configuring CloudMonkey

Problem

With CloudMonkey installed, you want to configure it with your API keys and your cloud endpoint.

Solution

Launch the CloudMonkey interactive shell and use the set command to define your endpoint and your keys. You can also edit the configuration file at ~/.cloudmonkey/ config and enter the values directly.

Discussion

To set up these values interactively from the CloudMonkey prompt, use the set command. The API and secretkeys are obtained via the CloudStack UI or via your cloud provider. You can use CloudMonkey to interact with a local cloud, and even with a remote public cloud. You just need to set the host, port, protocol, and keys properly. For instance, with CloudStack running locally, do the following:

```
$ cloudmonkey
☁ Apache CloudStack cloudmonkey 4.1.0-snapshot. Type help or ? to list commands.

> set prompt myprompt>
myprompt> set host localhost
myprompt> set port 8080
myprompt> set protocol http
myprompt> set apikey <your api key>
myprompt> set secretkey <your secret key>
```

To configure CloudMonkey, you can also edit the ~/.cloudmonkey/config file in the user's home directory as shown here (the values can also be set interactively at the cloudmon key prompt; logs are kept in ~/.cloudmonkey/log, history is stored in ~/.cloudmonkey/ history, and discovered APIs are listed in ~/.cloudmonkey/cache):

```
$ cat ~/.cloudmonkey/config
[core]
log_file = /Users/sebastiengoasguen/.cloudmonkey/log
asyncblock = true
paramcompletion = false
history_file = /Users/sebastiengoasguen/.cloudmonkey/history

[ui]
color = true
prompt = >
display = table

[user]
secretkey =VDaACYb0LV9eNjTetIOElcVQkvJck_J_QljX_FcHR
apikey = plgWJfZK4gyS3mOMTVmjUVg-X-jlWlnfaUJ9GAbBbf9

[server]
path = /client/api
host = localhost
protocol = http
```

```
port = 8080
timeout = 3600
```

The number of key/value pairs returned by the API calls can be large, resulting in a very long output. To enable easier viewing of the output, you can use a tabular display. You can even choose your set of column fields with a filter.

To enable it, use the set function to change the display value and create filters like so:

```
> set display table
> list users filter=id,domain,account
count = 1
user:
+--------------------------------------+--------+---------+
|                  id                  | domain | account |
+--------------------------------------+--------+---------+
| 7ed6d5da-93b2-4545-a502-23d20b48ef2a | ROOT   | admin   |
+--------------------------------------+--------+---------+
```

3.5. Using CloudMonkey as an Interactive Shell

Problem

You have installed and configured CloudMonkey, and you now want to explore the available API calls and get some information on the API call parameters.

Solution

Start the interactive shell and use the tab autocompletion feature to discover the API. Use the help functionality to list the parameters that a specific API needs, including the mandatory and optional parameters.

Discussion

The best way to start learning CloudMonkey is to use the interactive shell. Simply type **cloudMonkey** at the prompt to set the configuration parameters.

At the CloudMonkey prompt, press the Tab key twice; you will see all potential verbs available. Pick one, enter a space, and then press Tab twice. You will see all actions available for that verb.

By picking one action (e.g., create network) and entering a space plus the Tab key, you will obtain the list of parameters for that specific API call:

```
cloudmonkey>create network
account=             domainid=       isAsync=
networkdomain=       projectid=      vlan=
acltype=             endip=          name=
networkofferingid=   startip=        vpcid=
```

```
displaytext=        gateway=         netmask=
physicalnetworkid=  subdomainaccess= zoneid=
```

To get additional help on that specific API call, you can use the `-h`, `--help`, or `-help` options. The result will be the list of arguments for that call. Specifically, you will see the list of required arguments and the list of optional ones:

```
cloudmonkey>create network -h
Creates a network
Required args: displaytext name networkofferingid zoneid
Args: account acltype displaytext domainid endip gateway isAsync
name netmask networkdomain networkofferingid physicalnetworkid
projectid startip subdomainaccess vlan vpcid zoneid
```

 To find out the required parameters value, using a debugger console on the CloudStack UI might be very useful. For instance, using Firebug on Firefox, you can navigate the UI and check the parameters values for each call you are making as you navigate the UI.

3.6. Starting a Virtual Machine Instance with CloudMonkey

Problem

CloudMonkey can perform every CloudStack API call. You want to start an instance in your cloud.

Solution

Use the `deploy virtualmachine` call and pass a zone ID, a template ID, and a service offering ID as parameters. To obtain those IDs, you make other calls using CloudMonkey.

Discussion

To start a virtual machine instance (what I call the "Hello, world" of cloud), we will use the `deploy virtualmachine` API call:

```
cloudmonkey>deploy virtualmachine -h
Creates and automatically starts a virtual machine based
on a service offering, disk offering, and template.
Required args: serviceofferingid templateid zoneid
Args: account diskofferingid displayname domainid group hostid
hypervisor ipaddress iptonetworklist isAsync keyboard keypair
name networkids projectid securitygroupids securitygroupnames
serviceofferingid size startvm templateid userdata zoneid
```

The required arguments are `serviceofferingid`, `templateid`, and `zoneid`.

In order to specify the template that we want to use, we can list all available templates with the following call:

```
> list templates filter=id,displaytext templatefilter=executable
  count = 36
  template:
  +-------------------------------------+--------------------------------+
  |                id                   |          displaytext           |
  +-------------------------------------+--------------------------------+
  | 3235e860-2f00-416a-9fac-79a03679ffd8 | Windows Server 2012 R2 WINRM   |
  | 20d4ebc3-8898-431c-939e-adbcf203acec |  Linux Ubuntu 13.10 64-bit     |
  | 70d31a38-c030-490b-bca9-b9383895ade7 |  Linux Ubuntu 13.10 64-bit     |
  | 4822b64b-418f-4d6b-b64e-1517bb862511 |  Linux Ubuntu 13.10 64-bit     |
  | 39bc3611-5aea-4c83-a29a-7455298241a7 |  Linux Ubuntu 13.10 64-bit     |
...<snipped>
```

 The IDs that you will use will differ from this example. Make sure you use the ones that correspond to your CloudStack cloud. In this snippet, I used exoscale (*http://exoscale.ch*) and only showed the beginning output of the first template. Depending on your cloud provider, you will see a different output.

Similar to getting the `serviceofferingid`, you would do the following:

```
> list serviceofferings filter=id,name
  count = 7
  serviceoffering:
  +-------------------------------------+-------------+
  |                id                   |    name     |
  +-------------------------------------+-------------+
  | 71004023-bb72-4a97-b1e9-bc66dfce9470 |    Micro    |
  | b6cd1ff5-3a2f-4e9d-a4d1-8988c1191fe8 |    Tiny     |
  | 21624abb-764e-4def-81d7-9fc54b5957fb |    Small    |
  | b6e9d1e8-89fc-4db3-aaa4-9b4c5b1d0844 |   Medium    |
  | c6f99499-7f59-4138-9427-a09db13af2bc |    Large    |
  | 350dc5ea-fe6d-42ba-b6c0-efb8b75617ad | Extra-large |
  | a216b0d1-370f-4e21-a0eb-3dfc6302b564 |    Huge     |
  +-------------------------------------+-------------+
```

Note that we can use the Linux pipe as well as standard Linux commands within the interactive shell. Finally, we would start an instance with the following call:

```
cloudmonkey>deploy virtualmachine templateid=20d4ebc3-8898-431c-939e-adbcf203acec
    zoneid=1128bd56-b4d9-4ac6-a7b9-c715b187ce11
    serviceofferingid=71004023-bb72-4a97-b1e9-bc66dfce9470
    id = 5566c27c-e31c-438e-9d97-c5d5904453dc
    jobid = 334fbc33-c720-46ba-a710-182af31e76df
```

This is an asynchronous API call which returns a jobid. You can query the status of the job with the queryAsyncJobresult API:

```
> query asyncjobresult jobid=334fbc33-c720-46ba-a710-182af31e76df
    accountid = b8c0baab-18a1-44c0-ab67-e24049212925
    cmd = com.cloud.api.commands.DeployVMCmd
    created = 2014-03-05T13:40:18+0100
    jobid = 334fbc33-c720-46ba-a710-182af31e76df
    jobinstanceid = 5566c27c-e31c-438e-9d97-c5d5904453dc
    jobinstancetype = VirtualMachine
    jobprocstatus = 0
    jobresultcode = 0
    jobstatus = 0
    userid = 968f6b4e-b382-4802-afea-dd731d4cf9b9
```

Once the machine is being deployed you can list it:

```
> list virtualmachines filter=id,displayname
count = 1
virtualmachine:
+-----------------------------------------+-------------+
|                    id                   | displayname |
+-----------------------------------------+-------------+
| 5566c27c-e31c-438e-9d97-c5d5904453dc | foobar      |
+-----------------------------------------+-------------+
```

The instance can be stopped and you would see a different state when listing the virtual machines:

```
> stop virtualmachine id=5566c27c-e31c-438e-9d97-c5d5904453dc
jobid = 391b4666-293c-442b-8a16-aeb64eef0246

> list virtualmachines filter=id,state
count = 1
virtualmachine:
+-----------------------------------------+---------+
|                    id                   | state   |
+-----------------------------------------+---------+
| 5566c27c-e31c-438e-9d97-c5d5904453dc | Stopped |
+-----------------------------------------+---------+
```

Depending on your CloudStack setup, create a sshkeypair with create sshkeypair, a securitygroup with create securitygroup, and add some rules to it. Enjoy Cloud-Monkey as it is a very nice tool that provides support for the entire CloudStack API.

3.7. Using Apache Libcloud with CloudStack

Apache Libcloud (*http://libcloud.apache.org*) is another Python-based client that you can use to interact with the CloudStack API. Where CloudMonkey provides 100% API coverage, Libcloud only provides a small subset of that API. Its aim is to be a common API that abstracts all the differences between cloud providers' APIs. Libcloud supports over 20 cloud providers, and therefore the base libcloud API represents the lowest common denominator among all of them.

The CloudStack driver in libcloud is actively maintained and used by companies like SixSq (*http://sixsq.com*), CloudControl (*http://www.cloudcontrol.com*), and Cloudify (*http://cloudifysource.org*). It is a good choice if you are looking for a Python binding and trying to build an application that interacts with multiple cloud providers (e.g., CloudStack, OpenStack, AWS EC2, Google GCE).

Documentation for libcloud (*http://docs.libcloud.apache.org/en/latest/*) is quite complete and the community strives to keep it up to date. Check the CloudStack-driver-specific documentation (*http://bit.ly/driver-specific*) for a deeper dive into the methods available.

Problem

You are looking for a Python module to write scripts that automate tasks in your Cloud-Stack cloud. In addition, you need this Python module to support other types of cloud because you are interested in using a single API in your multiclouds application.

Solution

Install Apache Libcloud, a Python module that provides a single API for over 25 cloud providers. Libcloud supports the basic compute functionality on cloud providers like Rackspace, Google GCE, and AWS EC2, but also storage and load-balancing APIs. Using your API keys and endpoint, create a Driver object by instantiating the CloudStack provider class. You can then access the base libcloud API to list images, machine types, locations, and more.

Discussion

If you are familiar with PyPI, installing libcloud is as simple as:

```
$ sudo pip install apache-libcloud
```

A successful installation should allow you to import the libcloud module within a Python interactive shell:

```
$ python
Python 2.7.6 (default, Nov 12 2013, 13:26:39)
[GCC 4.2.1 Compatible Apple Clang 4.1 ((tags/Apple/clang-421.11.66))] on darwin
Type "help", "copyright", "credits" or "license" for more information.
>>> import libcloud
>>>
```

Developers who want to check the code behind the CloudStack driver might want to clone the repository. You can choose whether you want to clone from the GitHub mirror:

```
$ git clone https://github.com/apache/libcloud.git
```

or the Apache source repository:

```
$ git clone https://git-wip-us.apache.org/repos/asf/libcloud.git
```

If you have cloned the repository, you install libcloud with:

```
$ cd libcloud
$ sudo python ./setup.py install
```

 The CloudStack driver is located in */path/to/libcloud/source/libcloud/ compute/drivers/cloudstack.py*. You can file bugs on the libcloud JIRA (*http://bit.ly/libcloud_JIRA*); bug reports are very welcome.

With libcloud installed either via PyPI or via the source, you can now open a Python interactive shell, create an instance of the CloudStack driver, and call the available methods via the libcloud API. You will need to know the endpoint of the CloudStack API server and your API keys. You can reuse the one from Recipe 3.4.

First, you need to import the libcloud modules and create a CloudStack driver:

```
>>> from libcloud.compute.types import Provider
>>> from libcloud.compute.providers import get_driver
>>> Driver = get_driver(Provider.CLOUDSTACK)
```

Then, using your keys and endpoint, create a connection object. Note that this is a local test and thus not secured. If you use a CloudStack public cloud, make sure to use SSL properly (i.e., secure=True):

```
>>> apikey='plgWJfZK4gyS3mlZLYq_u38zCm0bewzGUdP66mg'
>>> secretkey='VDaACYb0LV9eNjeq1EhwJaw7FF3akA3KBQ'
>>> host='http://localhost:8080'
>>> path='/client/api'
>>> conn=Driver(key=apikey,secret=secretkey,secure=False,host='localhost', \
...port='8080',path=path)
```

To explore the available methods, you can type help(conn) at the Python shell, which will give you access to the CloudStack-specific methods and the associate docstrings. With the connection object in hand, you now use the libcloud base API (*http://bit.ly/ libcloud_base_API*) to list such things as the templates (i.e., images) and the service offerings (i.e., sizes). Python lists are returned, where each element in the list is an instance of an image and a size class:

```
>>> conn.list_images()
[<NodeImage: id=13ccff62-132b-4caf-b456-e8ef20cbff0e,
 name=tiny Linux, driver=CloudStack  ..>]
>>> conn.list_sizes()
[<NodeSize: id=ef2537ad-c70f-11e1-821b-0800277e749c,
```

```
name=tinyOffering, ram=100 disk=0 bandwidth=0 price=0 driver=CloudStack ..>,
<NodeSize: id=c66c2557-12a7-4b32-94f4-48837da3fa84,
name=Small Instance, ram=512 disk=0 bandwidth=0 price=0 driver=CloudStack ..>,
<NodeSize: id=3d8b82e5-d8e7-48d5-a554-cf853111bc50,
name=Medium Instance, ram=1024 disk=0 bandwidth=0 price=0 driver=CloudStack ..>]
```

The create_node method is used to start a virtual machine. Under the covers, the driver makes use of the deployVirtualMachine API that we have seen in CloudMonkey. create_node will take an instance name, a template, and an instance type as arguments. It will return an instance of a CloudStackNode that has some attributes and additional extensions methods, such as ex_stop and ex_start:

```
>>> images=conn.list_images()
>>> offerings=conn.list_sizes()
>>> node=conn.create_node(name='foobar',image=images[0],size=offerings[0])
>>> help(node)
>>> node.get_uuid()
'b1aa381ba1de7f2d5048e248848993d5a900984f'
>>> node.name
u'foobar'
```

This gives you a brief idea of what you can do with Apache Libcloud and how you use it. Although the base API is quite small, as soon as most drivers have an implementation of a similar functionality, the libcloud community tries to unify the methods being used. Recently, the management of SSH key pairs used to access the instances has been promoted to the base API. It is very likely that the management of security groups will also be incorporated in the base API.

3.8. Managing Key Pairs and Security Groups Using Libcloud

Problem

You have a CloudStack cloud that makes use of SSH key pairs and security groups. You want to list/create/delete key pairs as well as list/create/delete security groups and authorize some inbound traffic in those security groups.

Solution

You use the key pairs libcloud API calls, which are part of the base libcloud API. And you use the extension methods (with the ex- prefix) to manage your security groups.

Discussion

In public clouds like Amazon EC2, the use of SSH key pairs (*http://bit.ly/key_pairs*) is the de facto standard to access instances. CloudStack also supports this method of accessing instances and thankfully, `libcloud` too. Let's look at an example. Given a `conn` object obtained from the previous interactive session, you can list, create, and delete key pairs:

```
conn.list_key_pairs()
conn.create_key_pair(name='foobar')
conn.delete_key_pair(name='foobar')
```

Management of security groups is also available, but as mentioned, is not part of the base API. Instead it is available as so-called extension methods that have the `ex_` prefix. Here we show how to list, create, and delete a security group, as well as add an ingress rule to open port 22 to the world (both key pair and security groups are essential for access to a CloudStack basic zone like exoscale (*http://www.exoscale.ch*) and other public clouds like Amazon EC2):

```
conn.ex_list_security_groups()
conn.ex_create_security_group(name='libcloud')
conn.ex_authorize_security_group_ingress(securitygroupname='libcloud',
                                         protocol='TCP',startport=22,
                                         cidrlist='0.0.0.0/0')
conn.ex_delete_security_group('libcloud')
```

While these two functionalities are very interesting for Amazon-like public clouds, there is also support in the `libcloud` CloudStack driver for advanced zones. You can list networks, start instances in an advanced zone, and set up port forwarding rules as well as IP forwarding rules.

3.9. Hybrid Cloud Applications Using Libcloud

Problem

You want to write an application that accesses an on-premise CloudStack cloud and a public cloud like AWS EC2. This could be the case when you have some hybrid cloud setup—for example, with CloudStack being used to run stable workloads on-premise, and EC2 being used for burst compute needs.

Solution

You use `libcloud` because you know it supports many cloud providers, including CloudStack, EC2, and GCE. Using your API keys for the clouds you want to use, you create connection objects using the appropriate provider and iterate over those two drivers. The base `libcloud` API will be common to both drivers.

Discussion

One of the interesting use cases of Libcloud is that you can use multiple cloud providers, (e.g., AWS, Rackspace, OpenNebula, vCloud, etc.). You can then create driver instances to each of these clouds and create your own multicloud application. In the following example, we instantiate the libcloud CloudStack driver on exoscale (*http://exoscale.ch*) and the Amazon EC2 driver in the US WEST region. We then print the location of each zone the drivers are connected to as well as the list of SSH key pairs existing in each cloud:

```
#!/usr/bin/env python

import os

from libcloud.compute.types import import Provider
from libcloud.compute.providers import get_driver

apikey=os.getenv('EXOSCALE_API_KEY')
secretkey=os.getenv('EXOSCALE_SECRET_KEY')
Driver = get_driver(Provider.EXOSCALE)
exoconn=Driver(key=apikey,secret=secretkey)

apikey = os.getenv('AWSAccessKeyId')
secretkey = os.getenv('AWSSecretKey')
Driver = get_driver(Provider.EC2_US_WEST)
ec2conn = Driver(ACCESS_ID, SECRET_KEY)

drivers = [exoconn, ec2conn]
for driver in drivers:
    print driver.list_locations()
    print driver.list_key_pairs()
```

From this basic setup, you can imagine how you would write an application that would manage instances in different cloud providers. In this example, you might also notice that we instantiated the exoscale driver a bit differently than in Recipe 3.8. Indeed, libcloud also implements CloudStack-specific cloud providers. This means that there are definitions for existing public clouds that are based on CloudStack, like exoscale (*http://exoscale.ch*), iKoula (*http://ikoula.com*), and the Korean Telecom cloud KTU-Cloud (*http://ucloudbiz.olleh.com*).

3.10. IPython Interactive Shell with Libcloud

Problem

Writing Python scripts to interact with your cloud can be error prone. You are looking for an interactive shell that is similar to CloudMonkey but that you can use with multiple clouds.

Solution

Using libcloud and IPython, create an interactive shell that contains an instantiated driver to your cloud. You can then explore the libcloud API with the nice tab completion feature of IPython, log all your commands for rapid prototyping, and much more.

Discussion

To wrap up this quick tour of libcloud, I want to leave you with a fully working example of an interactive shell to exoscale (*http://exoscale.ch*). It makes use of IPython, which you will need to install. Using pip, you can install it with one command:

```
$ sudo pip install ipython
```

I find it extremely useful, because IPython brings logging capability, tab completion, as well as history. These simple features can come in handy when doing debugging/testing work. Using IPython requires an account on exoscale, and you have to store your keys as environment variables:

```
#!/usr/bin/env python

import sys
import os

from IPython.terminal.embed import InteractiveShellEmbed

from libcloud.compute.types import Provider
from libcloud.compute.providers import get_driver

apikey=os.getenv('EXOSCALE_API_KEY')
secretkey=os.getenv('EXOSCALE_SECRET_KEY')

Driver = get_driver(Provider.EXOSCALE)

conn=Driver(key=apikey,secret=secretkey)

shell = InteractiveShellEmbed(banner1="Hello from Libcloud Shell!")
shell()
```

Copy this script to your local machine and execute it, and you will have an interactive shell prompt. Loaded in this shell will be the conn object that contains all the libcloud methods available for CloudStack.

3.11. Installing and Configuring jclouds CLI

jclouds (*http://jclouds.apache.org*) is a Java wrapper for many cloud providers' APIs. It is used in a large number of cloud applications to access providers that do not offer a standard API. jclouds is similar to the libcloud philosophy in that it aims to offer a common API that abstracts the differences in cloud providers' APIs. It solves the standard issue without defining one. `jclouds-cli` is a command-line interface that uses jclouds. It could be seen as an equivalent to CloudMonkey.

However, CloudMonkey covers the entire CloudStack API and `jclouds-cli` does not. It offers basic functionality for managing virtual machines plus management of blobstore (i.e., S3 like) and configuration management via Chef. You should see it as an example of what you can do with jclouds without being a Java developer.

 jclouds is a top-level project at the Apache Software Foundation. `jclouds-cli` is not part of the jclouds official ASF release but is available on GitHub. Development activity may have slowed down.

Problem

You are a Java developer looking for a cloud API abstraction layer that allows you to develop applications that use multiple clouds (public or private).

Solution

Use Apache jclouds (*https://jclouds.apache.org/*), a Java toolkit that allows you to build applications that are portable among clouds. The Apache jclouds website describes the toolkit as follows:

> Apache jclouds is an open source multi-cloud toolkit for the Java platform that gives you the freedom to create applications that are portable across clouds while giving you full control to use cloud-specific features.

Discussion

To give you a taste of jclouds, we are going to install and configure the jclouds command-line interface.

First, clone `jclouds-cli` from GitHub and build it with Maven—the same maven that we used to build CloudStack (yes, it's a Java project):

```
$ git clone https://github.com/jclouds/jclouds-cli.git
$ cd jclouds-cli
$ mvn install
```

Now, find the tarball generated by the build in *assembly/target*, extract the tarball in the directory of your choice, and add the *bin* directory to your path. For instance:

```
$ export PATH=/Users/sebastiengoasguen/Documents/jclouds-cli-1.7.0/bin
```

You then define a few environmental variables to set your cloud endpoint and your credentials (i.e., API and secret keys). The ones listed here are just examples, so adapt to your own endpoint and keys, as you did before:

```
$ export JCLOUDS_COMPUTE_API=cloudstack
$ export JCLOUDS_COMPUTE_ENDPOINT=http://localhost:8080/client/api
$ export JCLOUDS_COMPUTE_CREDENTIAL=_UKIzPgw7BneOyJO621Tdlslicg
$ export JCLOUDS_COMPUTE_IDENTITY=mnH5EbKcKeJdJrvguEIwQG_Fn-N0l
```

You should now be able to use jclouds-cli. Check that it is in your path and runs; you should see the following output:

```
sebmini:jclouds-cli-1.7.0-SNAPSHOT sebastiengoasguen$ jclouds-cli
```

```
    jclouds cli (1.7.0-SNAPSHOT)
    http://jclouds.org

Hit '<tab>' for a list of available commands
and '[cmd] --help' for help on a specific command.
Hit '<ctrl-d>' to shutdown jclouds cli.

jclouds> features:list
State          Version          Name                 Repository
[installed  ] [1.7.0-SNAPSHOT] jclouds-guice        jclouds-1.7.0-SNAPSHOT
[installed  ] [1.7.0-SNAPSHOT] jclouds              jclouds-1.7.0-SNAPSHOT
[installed  ] [1.7.0-SNAPSHOT] jclouds-blobstore    jclouds-1.7.0-SNAPSHOT
[installed  ] [1.7.0-SNAPSHOT] jclouds-compute      jclouds-1.7.0-SNAPSHOT
[installed  ] [1.7.0-SNAPSHOT] jclouds-management   jclouds-1.7.0-SNAPSHOT
[uninstalled] [1.7.0-SNAPSHOT] jclouds-api-filesystem jclouds-1.7.0-SNAPSHOT
[installed  ] [1.7.0-SNAPSHOT] jclouds-aws-ec2      jclouds-1.7.0-SNAPSHOT
[uninstalled] [1.7.0-SNAPSHOT] jclouds-aws-route53  jclouds-1.7.0-SNAPSHOT
[installed  ] [1.7.0-SNAPSHOT] jclouds-aws-s3       jclouds-1.7.0-SNAPSHOT
[uninstalled] [1.7.0-SNAPSHOT] jclouds-aws-sqs      jclouds-1.7.0-SNAPSHOT
[uninstalled] [1.7.0-SNAPSHOT] jclouds-aws-sts      jclouds-1.7.0-SNAPSHOT
...<snip>
```

You are now up and running with jclouds-cli. Congratulations!

I edited the output of jclouds-cli to gain some space. There are a lot more providers available.

3.12. Using jclouds CLI with CloudStack

Problem

You have installed and configured the jclouds CLI and want to use it with your Cloud-Stack cloud to start instances.

Solution

Obtain the uuid of the image you want to use with the `jclouds image list` command. Obtain the uuid of the machine type you want to use with the `jclouds hardware list` command. Finally, start an instance with the `jclouds node create` command.

Discussion

The CloudStack API driver is not installed by default. Install it with the following:

```
jclouds> features:install jclouds-api-cloudstack
```

For now, we will only test the virtual machine management functionality. Pretty basic, but that's what we want to do to get a feel for `jclouds-cli`. If you have set your endpoint and keys properly, you should be able to list the location of your cloud like so:

```
$ jclouds location list
[id]                            [scope]  [description]              [parent]
cloudstack                      PROVIDER https://api.exoscale.ch/compute
1128bd56-b4d9-4ac6-a7b9-c715 ZONE    CH-GV2                        cloudstack
```

Again, this is an example. You will see something different depending on your endpoint.

You can list the service offerings as follows:

```
$ jclouds hardware list
[id]                            [ram]   [cpu] [cores]
71004023-bb72-4a97-b1e9-bc66dfce9470   512   2198.0   1.0
b6cd1ff5-3a2f-4e9d-a4d1-8988c1191fe8  1024   2198.0   1.0
21624abb-764e-4def-81d7-9fc54b5957fb  2048   4396.0   2.0
b6e9d1e8-89fc-4db3-aaa4-9b4c5b1d0844  4096   4396.0   2.0
c6f99499-7f59-4138-9427-a09db13af2bc  8182   8792.0   4.0
350dc5ea-fe6d-42ba-b6c0-efb8b75617ad 16384   8792.0   4.0
a216b0d1-370f-4e21-a0eb-3dfc6302b564 32184  17584.0   8.0
```

List the images available with the following:

```
$ jclouds image list
[id]                            [location] [os family]  [os version] [status]
0f9f4f49-afc2-4139-b26b-b05a9              windows      null         AVAILABLE
1d16c78d-268f-47d0-be0c-b80d3              unrecognized null         AVAILABLE
3cfd96dc-acce-4423-a095-e558f              unrecognized null         AVAILABLE
...<snip>
```

We see that the OS family is not listed properly, probably due to some regex used by jclouds to guess the OS type. Unfortunately, the name is not given.

To start an instance, we can check the syntax of `jclouds node create`:

```
$ jclouds node create --help
DESCRIPTION
        jclouds:node-create

    Creates a node.

SYNTAX
        jclouds:node-create [options] group [number]

ARGUMENTS
        group
                Node group.
        number
                Number of nodes to create.
                (defaults to 1)
```

We need to define the name of a group and give the number of the instance that we want to start, plus the hardware and image ID. In terms of hardware, we are going to use the smallest possible hardware, and for image, we give a `uuid` from the previous list. To list the running instances, `jclouds node list` will do the trick, and to get more information about a specific node, `jclouds node info` will be your friend:

```
$ jclouds node create --ImageId 1d16c78d-268f-47d0-be0c-b80d31e765d2
                      --smallest foobar 1
$ jclouds node info 4e733609-4c4a-4de1-9063-6fe5800ccb10
```

And that's pretty much what `jclouds-cli` is about. With this short intro, you are well on your way to using `jclouds-cli`. You may prefer it to CloudMonkey or Libcloud. If you are a Java developer, it might be a better platform to build on. CloudStack does not provide an object store, so the blobstore functionality is not going to be useful to us. Check out the interactive shell, the blobstore, and the chef facility to automate VM configuration. Remember that jclouds is actually foremost a Java library that you can use to write other applications. You can use jclouds directly without making use of this CLI.

3.13. Using CloStack: A Clojure Client for CloudStack

CloStack is a Clojure client for Apache CloudStack. Clojure (*http://clojure.org*) is a dynamic programming language for the Java Virtual Machine (JVM). It is compiled directly in JVM bytecode but offers the dynamic and interactive nature of an interpreted language like Python. Clojure is a dialect of LISP and, as such, is mostly a functional programming language. Clojure is gaining a lot of traction recently, one reason among distributed computing folks being the coreasync library (*https://github.com/clojure/*

core.async), which makes writing efficient multithreaded applications extremely fast and concise. Pallet (*http://palletops.com*) is a good example of a software based on Clojure and built for cloud automation.

You can try Clojure in your browser (*http://tryclj.com*) and get familiar with its read-eval-print loop (REPL). To get started, you can follow the tutorial (*http://bit.ly/Clojure_tutorial*) for non-LISP programmers through this web-based REPL.

Problem

You are writing a Clojure project that needs to access a CloudStack cloud. You need a CloudStack client written in Clojure.

Solution

You use CloStack (*https://github.com/pyr/clostack.git*). Install Leiningen (*https://github.com/technomancy/leiningen*) and use the REPL to get familiar with the Clojure syntax if you are not already used to it. Install CloStack and use the REPL to make your first Clojure base calls to a CloudStack cloud.

Discussion

Leiningen (*https://github.com/technomancy/leiningen*) is a tool for managing Clojure projects easily. With `lein`, you can create the skeleton of Clojure project as well as start a REPL to test your code.

Installing the latest version of Leiningen is easy: get the script (*http://bit.ly/latest_Leiningen*), make it executable, and set it in your path. You are done.

The first time you run `lein repl`, it will boostrap itself:

```
$ lein repl
Downloading Leiningen to /Users/sebgoa/.lein/self-installs
                        /leiningen-2.3.4-standalone.jar now...
  % Total    % Received % Xferd  Average Speed   Time    Time     Time  Current
                                 Dload  Upload   Total   Spent    Left  Speed
100 13.0M  100 13.0M    0     0  1574k      0  0:00:08  0:00:08 --:--:-- 2266k
nREPL server started on port 58633 on host 127.0.0.1
REPL-y 0.3.0
Clojure 1.5.1
    Docs: (doc function-name-here)
          (find-doc "part-of-name-here")
  Source: (source function-name-here)
 Javadoc: (javadoc java-object-or-class-here)
    Exit: Control+D or (exit) or (quit)
 Results: Stored in vars *1, *2, *3, an exception in *e

user=> exit
Bye for now!
```

Now that you have your own Clojure REPL, get a taste for it. Here is how you would add 2 and 2:

```
user=> (+ 2 2)
4
```

And how you would define a function:

```
user=> (defn f [x y]
  #_=> (+ x y))
#'user/f
user=> (f 2 3)
5
```

This should give you a taste of functional programming. For more, check out Luke VanderHart and Ryan Neufeld's *Clojure Cookbook*, and Chas Emerick, Brian Carper, and Christophe Grand's *Clojure Programming*, both from O'Reilly.

Let's get started with CloStack. To install it, like we did with several packages already, clone the GitHub repository (*https://github.com/pyr/clostack.git*) and start lein repl:

```
$ git clone https://github.com/pyr/clostack.git
$ cd clostack
$ lein repl
<...snip...>
nREPL server started on port 58655 on host 127.0.0.1
REPL-y 0.3.0
Clojure 1.5.1
    Docs: (doc function-name-here)
          (find-doc "part-of-name-here")
  Source: (source function-name-here)
 Javadoc: (javadoc java-object-or-class-here)
    Exit: Control+D or (exit) or (quit)
 Results: Stored in vars *1, *2, *3, an exception in *e

user=> exit
```

The first time that you start the REPL, lein will download all the clostack dependencies. I skipped this in the example.

In order to make your first clostack call, export a few environment variables to define your cloud endpoint and your API keys:

```
$ export CLOUDSTACK_ENDPOINT=http://localhost:8080/client/api
$ export CLOUDSTACK_API_KEY=HGWEFHWERH8978yg98ysdfghsdfgsagf
$ export CLOUDSTACK_API_SECRET=fhdsfhdf869guh3guwghseruig
```

Then relaunch the REPL and import the clostack client:

```
$ lein repl
nREPL server started on port 59890 on host 127.0.0.1
REPL-y 0.3.0
Clojure 1.5.1
    Docs: (doc function-name-here)
```

```
             (find-doc "part-of-name-here")
   Source: (source function-name-here)
  Javadoc: (javadoc java-object-or-class-here)
     Exit: Control+D or (exit) or (quit)
  Results: Stored in vars *1, *2, *3, an exception in *e

user=> (use 'clostack.client)
SLF4J: Failed to load class "org.slf4j.impl.StaticLoggerBinder".
SLF4J: Defaulting to no-operation (NOP) logger implementation
SLF4J: See http://www.slf4j.org/codes.html#StaticLoggerBinder
       for further details.
nil
user=> (def cs (http-client))
#'user/cs
```

You can safely discard the warning message, which only indicates that clostack is meant to be used as a library in a Clojure project. Define a client to your CloudStack endpoint and make your first API call like so:

```
user=> (list-zones cs)
{:listzonesresponse {:count 1,
                     :zone [{:id "1128bd56-b4d9-4ac6-a7b9-c715b187ce11",
                             :name "CH-GV2", :networktype "Basic",
                             :securitygroupsenabled true,
                             :allocationstate "Enabled",
                             :zonetoken "ccb0a60c-79c8-3230",
                             :dhcpprovider "VirtualRouter",
                             :localstorageenabled true}]}}
```

To explore the API calls that you can make, the REPL features tab completion (just like CloudMonkey and the libcloud IPython shell). Enter list or de and press the Tab key. You should see the following:

```
user=> (list
list                            list*
list-capabilities               list-disk-offerings
list-firewall-rules             list-hypervisors
list-iso-permissions            list-isos
list-load-balancer-rules        list-network-ac-ls
list-os-categories              list-os-types
list-project-accounts           list-project-invitations
list-remote-access-vpns         list-resource-limits
list-snapshot-policies          list-snapshots
list-tags                       list-template-permissions
list-volumes                    list-vp-cs
list-vpn-customer-gateways      list-vpn-gateway
list?

user=> (de
dec                             dec'
default-data-readers            definline
defmulti                        defn
```

```
defrecord                         defreq
delay?                            delete-account-from-project
delete-iso                        delete-lb-stickiness-policy
delete-port-forwarding-rule       delete-project
delete-snapshot                   delete-snapshot-policies
delete-template                   delete-volume
delete-vpn-gateway                deliver
derive                            descendants
detach-volume
```

To pass arguments to a call, follow the syntax:

```
user=> (list-templates cs :templatefilter "executable")
```

By now, this should look very familiar to what you have done before, but the functional programming aspect of Clojure will throw you for a loop at first. Hang in there.

3.14. Starting a Virtual Machine with CloStack

Problem

You want to start a virtual machine in your cloud using CloStack.

Solution

Obtain the uuids of the zone, template, and service offering you want to use, and then call the deploy-virtual-machine function. You can query the status of this asynchronous job with the query-async-job function.

Discussion

To deploy a virtual machine, our litmus test of Cloud, you need to get the serviceof feringid or instance type, the templateid (also known as the image ID), and the zoneid. The call is then very similar to CloudMonkey and returns a jobid:

```
user=> (deploy-virtual-machine cs
        :serviceofferingid "71004023-bb72-4a97-b1e9-bc66dfce9470"
        :templateid "1d961c82-7c8c-4b84-b61b-601876dab8d0"
        :zoneid "1128bd56-b4d9-4ac6-a7b9-c715b187ce11")
{:deployvirtualmachineresponse {:id "d0a887d2-e20b-4b25-98b3-c2995e4e428a",
 :jobid "21d20b5c-ea6e-4881-b0b2-0c2f9f1fb6be"}}
```

You can pass additional parameters to the deploy-virtual-machine call, such as the keypair and the securitygroupname:

```
user=> (deploy-virtual-machine cs
        :serviceofferingid "71004023-bb72-4a97-b1e9-bc66dfce9470"
        :templateid "1d961c82-7c8c-4b84-b61b-601876dab8d0"
        :zoneid "1128bd56-b4d9-4ac6-a7b9-c715b187ce11"
        :keypair "exoscale")
```

```
{:deployvirtualmachineresponse {:id "b5fdc41f-e151-43e7-a036-4d87b8536408",
 :jobid "418026fc-1009-4e7a-9721-7c9ad47b49e4"}}
```

To query the asynchronous job, you can use the query-async-job API call:

```
user=> (query-async-job-result cs :jobid "418026fc-1009-4e7a-9721-7c9ad47b49e4")
{:queryasyncjobresultresponse {:jobid "418026fc-1009-4e7a-9721-7c9ad47b49e4",
 :jobprocstatus 0,
 :jobinstancetype "VirtualMachine",
 :accountid "b8c0baab-18a1-44c0-ab67-e24049212925",
 :jobinstanceid "b5fdc41f-e151-43e7-a036-4d87b8536408",
 :created "2013-12-16T12:25:21+0100",
 :jobstatus 0, :jobresultcode 0,
 :cmd "com.cloud.api.commands.DeployVMCmd",
 :userid "968f6b4e-b382-4802-afea-dd731d4cf9b9"}}
```

And finally, to destroy the virtual machine, you would pass the id of the VM to the destroy-virtual-machine call like so:

```
user=> (destroy-virtual-machine cs :id "d0a887d2-e20b-4b25-98b3-c2995e4e428a")
{:destroyvirtualmachineresponse {:jobid "8fc8a8cf-9b54-435c-945d-e3ea2f183935"}}
```

With these simple basics, you can keep on exploring clostack, and learn more about Clojure (*http://clojure.org*) and the CloudStack API.

3.15. Use CloStack Within Your Own Clojure project

Problem

You have set up Leiningen and cloned the Git repository of CloStack, you know how to deploy a virtual machine, and you are familiar with the Clojure syntax. Now you want to write your own Clojure project that uses the CloStack library.

Solution

Use lein to create the skeleton of a new project and edit the project dependencies to include CloStack as well as some logging libraries.

Discussion

Clostack is meant to be used as a library in a Clojure project. So how would you do it? Let's write a "Hello, World" in Clojure.

To write your own Clojure project that makes use of clostack, use lein to create a project skeleton:

```
$ lein new foobar
```

`lein` will automatically create a *src/foobar/core.clj* file; edit it to replace the function foobar with `-main`. This dummy function returns `Hello, world!`. Let's try to execute it. First, we will need to define the `main` namespace in the *project.clj* file. Edit it like so:

```
defproject foobar "0.1.0-SNAPSHOT"
  :description "FIXME: write description"
  :url "http://example.com/FIXME"
  :license {:name "Eclipse Public License"
            :url "http://www.eclipse.org/legal/epl-v10.html"}
  :main foobar.core
  :dependencies [[org.clojure/clojure "1.5.1"]])
```

Note the `:main foobar.core`.

You can now execute the code with `lein run john`. Indeed, if you check the `-main` function in *src/foobar/core.clj*, you will see that it takes an argument. Surprisingly, you should see the following output:

```
$ lein run john
john Hello, world!
```

Let's now add the CloStack dependency and modify the `main` function to return the zone of the CloudStack cloud.

Edit *project.clj* to add a dependency on `clostack` and a few logging packages:

```
:dependencies [[org.clojure/clojure "1.5.1"]
               [clostack "0.1.3"]
               [org.clojure/tools.logging "0.2.6"]
               [org.slf4j/slf4j-log4j12   "1.6.4"]
               [log4j/apache-log4j-extras "1.0"]
               [log4j/log4j               "1.2.16"]
                :exclusions [javax.mail/mail
                             javax.jms/jms
                             com.sun.jdkmk/jmxtools
                             com.sun.jmx/jmxri]]])
```

`lein` should have created a *resources* directory. In it, create a *log4j.properties* file like so:

```
$ more log4j.properties
# Root logger option
log4j.rootLogger=INFO, stdout

# Direct log messages to stdout
log4j.appender.stdout=org.apache.log4j.ConsoleAppender
log4j.appender.stdout.Target=System.out
log4j.appender.stdout.layout=org.apache.log4j.PatternLayout
log4j.appender.stdout.layout.ConversionPattern=%d{yyyy-MM-dd HH:mm:ss}
                                               %-5p %c{1}:%L - %m%n
```

A discussion on logging is beyond the scope of this recipe; we merely add it in the configuration for a complete example.

Now you can edit the code in *src/foobar/core.clj* with some basic calls:

```
(ns testclostack.core
  (:require [clostack.client :refer [http-client list-zones]]))

(defn foo
  "I don't do a whole lot."
  [x]
  (println x "Hello, world!"))

(def cs (http-client))

(defn -main [args]
  (println (list-zones cs))
  (println args "Hey Wassup")
  (foo args)
)
```

Simply run this Clojure code with `lein run joe` in the source of your project. And that's it—you have sucessfully discovered the very basics of Clojure and used the Cloud-Stack client `clostack` to write your first Clojure code.

 For something more significant, look at Pallet (*http://palletops.com*), which is a framework for configuration and automation of cloud resources orchestration. Pallet is developed in Clojure.

3.16. StackerBee, a Ruby Client for CloudStack

CloudMonkey (see Recipe 3.3) and Libcloud (see Recipe 3.7) are Python based, CloStack (see Recipe 3.13) is for Clojure, and jclouds (see Recipe 3.11) is for Java developers. If you want to use Ruby, you may want to try Fog (*http://fog.io*); however, support for the CloudStack API is lagging behind a bit. StackerBee (*https://github.com/promptworks/ stacker_bee*) is a new Ruby client that works with all versions of the CloudStack API.

Problem

Ruby is your favorite scripting language and you want to use it to automate some tasks on your cloud. You also find that Fog (*http://fog.io*) does not support the latest Cloud-Stack API.

Solution

Install the StackerBee Ruby gem and write a Ruby script that creates a connection object to your CloudStack endpoint. The CloudStack APIs will be available on that object, and you will be able to do everything you need.

Discussion

Install StackerBee in a single command:

```
$ sudo gem install stacker_bee
```

The StackerBee (*https://github.com/promptworks/stacker_bee*) website has a lot of good documentation on what can be done, including using a read-eval-print loop (REPL). Here we show a sample script that returns the names of the virtual machines and the names of the SSH key pairs (you could of course use the create APIs to create volumes, servers, key pairs, etc.):

```ruby
#!/usr/bin/env ruby

require 'stacker_bee'

cloud_stack = StackerBee::Client.new(
  url:        'https://api.exoscale.ch/compute',
  api_key:    '<your API key>',
  secret_key: '<your API secret key>',
  ssl_verify: false
)

vms = cloud_stack.list_virtual_machines()

vms.each { |vm| puts vm[:displayname] }

keys = cloud_stack.list_ssh_key_pairs()

keys.each { |key| puts key[:name] }
```

 A nice feature of StackerBee is that the API version is configurable. Using the listApis through CloudMonkey, you can obtain a JSON file that contains the description of all APIs available. StackerBee can use this JSON file to construct the available methods. Just set the api_path to the location of the JSON file containing all API responses:

```
StackerBee::Client.api_path = '/path/to/your/listApis/response.json'
```

## CHAPTER 4

API Interfaces

4.1. Installing and Configuring EC2Stack

CloudStack features a native EC2 query interface called `awsapi` that can be run on the management server. EC2Stack (*http://bit.ly/ec2stack*) is a new project by CloudStack committer Ian Duffy and his friend Darren Brogan from University College Dublin. They did this as part of their third-year school project. Building on their previous experience with `gstack` (*http://bit.ly/gstack*) (see Recipe 4.7), a GCE interface to CloudStack, they wrote a brand new EC2 interface to CloudStack.

The interface uses Flask (*http://flask.pocoo.org*) microframework and is written 100% in Python. It also features a Vagrant (*http://vagrantup.com*) box for easy testing, lots of unit tests, and automatic build tests (pep8, pylint and coverage) via Travis (*https://travis-ci.org*) CI. As part of Google Summer of Code 2014, Darren Brogan is enhancing EC2Stack with additional API and unit tests.

Problem

You want an AWS EC2 compliant interface to your CloudStack cloud in order to use AWS clients like the AWS CLI (*http://aws.amazon.com/cli/*) or Python Boto (Recipe 4.4).

Solution

Download EC2Stack from the Python package index or install it from source by cloning the GitHub repository.

Discussion

Install EC2Stack using `pip` in a single operation:

```
$ sudo pip install ec2stack
```

If you want to do it from source and check out the code, then clone the Git repository and install it by hand:

```
$ git clone https://github.com/BroganD1993/ec2stack.git
$ sudo python ./setup.py install
```

You will now have *ec2stack* and *ec2stack-configure* binaries in your path. Before running the application, you will need to configure it. As an example, to set it up with exoscale (*http://exoscale.ch*) do the following:

```
$ ec2stack-configure
EC2Stack bind address [0.0.0.0]:
EC2Stack bind port [5000]:
Cloudstack host [localhost]: api.exoscale.ch
Cloudstack port [8080]: 443
Cloudstack protocol [http]: https
Cloudstack path [/client/api]: /compute
Cloudstack custom disk offering name [Custom]:
Cloudstack default zone name: CH-GV2
Do you wish to input instance type mappings? (Yes/No): Yes
Insert the AWS EC2 instance type you wish to map: m1.small
Insert the name of the instance type you wish to map this to: Tiny
Do you wish to add more mappings? (Yes/No): No
INFO  [alembic.migration] Context impl SQLiteImpl.
INFO  [alembic.migration] Will assume non-transactional DDL.
```

 Note that we created a mapping between the AWS m1.small instance type and the Tiny instance type in exoscale. You could add more mappings.

You are now ready to run ec2stack. This setup process will run the application on the foreground. Because it is a Flask application, you can deploy it as a service in several ways. The Flask Documentation (*http://bit.ly/flask_docs*) has good tips to do this. For testing, you can run it in the foreground; EC2Stack will be listening for requests and be ready to forward them to your CloudStack cloud:

```
$ ec2stack
 * Running on http://0.0.0.0:5000/
 * Restarting with reloader
```

4.2. Using the AWS CLI with EC2Stack

Problem

With EC2Stack running, you want to use the AWS CLI (*http://aws.amazon.com/cli/*) to make calls to your CloudStack cloud.

Solution

Install the AWS CLI from PyPI (*https://pypi.python.org/pypi/awscli*) and configure it. Register your API keys with EC2Stack and start making requests to your cloud.

Discussion

Now that you are running EC2Stack on your local machine, you can use the AWS CLI to make calls to it. Install the CLI with:

```
$ sudo pip install awscli
```

 The Python AWS CLI available on PyPI may change often (*http://aws.amazon.com/releasenotes/CLI*), which can cause EC2Stack to break. You can install a specific awscli package with:

```
$ sudo pip install awscli==1.3.10
```

Currently, EC2Stack stack has been tested with 1.3.10.

In addition, you need to register your API keys with the AWS CLI. If you have not used exoscale (as in the preceding example), then choose the keys of your own CloudStack deployment and use the appropriate region name:

```
$ aws configure
AWS Access Key ID [None]: PQogHs2sk_3uslfvrASjQFDlZbt0mEDd14iN
AWS Secret Access Key [None]: aHuDB2ewpgxVuQlvD9P1o313BioI1W4v
Default region name [None]: CH-GV2
Default output format [None]:
```

You can see these settings in the *~/.aws/config* file. Check the AWS CLI reference (*http://docs.aws.amazon.com/cli/latest/reference/*) for further customization. The output format can be json, text, or table.

With your AWS CLI installed and configured, the final configuration step is to register a user with EC2Stack. To be on the safe side, upgrade the requests module:

```
$ sudo pip install --upgrade requests
```

Register your API keys like so:

```
$ ec2stack-register http://localhost:5000 <API accesskey> <API secret key>
```

The command should return a Successfully Registered! message. At this stage, you are now ready to use the AWS CLI (or Boto) and send requests to the EC2Stack endpoint:

```
$ aws ec2 describe-images --endpoint=http://localhost:5000
$ aws ec2 describe-key-pairs --endpoint=http://localhost:5000
$ aws ec2 create-key-pair --endpoint=http://localhost:5000 --key-name=test
```

To start an instance, for example:

```
$ aws ec2 run-instances --image-id=20d4ebc3-8898-431c-939e-adbcf203acec
 --endpoint=http://localhost:5000
```

The `image-id` parameter is the CloudStack uuid corresponding to the template that you want to start. You find it by running the `aws describe-images` call.

4.3. Improving the EC2Stack API Coverage

Problem

The EC2Stack API coverage does not cover all the AWS EC2 API. You want to add an API.

Solution

Because EC2Stack is open source, you can easily contribute to it and add the API that you need. Fork the project on GitHub (*http://bit.ly/_ec2stack*) and submit a pull request.

Discussion

Looking at the code (*http://bit.ly/covered_APIs*), only the following AWS APIs are covered (more are being added through a Google Summer of Code 2014 project):

```
def _get_action(action):
    actions = {
    'AttachVolume': volumes.attach_volume,
    'AuthorizeSecurityGroupEgress':
     security_groups.authenticate_security_group_egress,
    'AuthorizeSecurityGroupIngress':
     security_groups.authenticate_security_group_ingress,
    'CreateKeyPair': keypairs.create_keypair,
    'CreateSecurityGroup': security_groups.create_security_group,
    'CreateTags': tags.create_tags,
    'CreateVolume': volumes.create_volume,
    'DeleteKeyPair': keypairs.delete_keypair,
    'DeleteSecurityGroup': security_groups.delete_security_group,
    'DeleteTags': tags.delete_tags,
    'DeleteVolume': volumes.delete_volume,
    'DescribeAvailabilityZones': zones.describe_zones,
    'DescribeImageAttribute': images.describe_image_attribute,
    'DescribeImages': images.describe_images,
    'DescribeInstanceAttribute': instances.describe_instance_attribute,
    'DescribeInstances': instances.describe_instances,
    'DescribeKeyPairs': keypairs.describe_keypairs,
    'DescribeSecurityGroups': security_groups.describe_security_groups,
    'DescribeTags': tags.describe_tags,
    'DescribeVolumes': volumes.describe_volumes,
    'DetachVolume': volumes.detach_volume,
    'GetPasswordData': passwords.get_password_data,
```

```
'ImportKeyPair': keypairs.import_keypair,
'RebootInstances': instances.reboot_instance,
'RegisterSecretKey': register_secret_key,
'RemoveSecretKey': remove_secret_key,
'RevokeSecurityGroupEgress':
 security_groups.revoke_security_group_egress,
'RevokeSecurityGroupIngress':
 security_groups.revoke_security_group_ingress,
'RunInstances': instances.run_instance,
'StartInstances': instances.start_instance,
'StopInstances': instances.stop_instance,
'TerminateInstances': instances.terminate_instance,
    }
```

Currently, EC2Stack is geared toward CloudStack basic zones. It is aimed at clouds that resemble AWS EC2 and want to allow access via SSH key pairs and security groups. Virtual private clouds (VPCs) are not currently supported.

The code is quite clean and it will be easy to add more actions and provide a much better coverage really soon. Pull requests are welcome if you are interested to contribute.

4.4. Using Python Boto with EC2Stack

There are many tools available to interface with an AWS-compatible API. In the previous recipe, we saw how to use the AWS CLI, but now let's briefly look at Boto. Boto is a Python package (*https://github.com/boto/boto*) that provides client-side bindings to work with the AWS API. It interfaces with EC2 but also with S3, CF, EMR, and so on. Boto has extensive documentation (*http://boto.readthedocs.org/en/latest/*) for each AWS service it supports.

Problem

You are familiar with Boto and want to use it with your CloudStack cloud.

Solution

Install Boto from the Python Package Index, and install and run an AWS EC2 interface to CloudStack. Write a Python script that imports the Boto module and creates a connection object to your EC2 interface endpoint.

Discussion

Installation is as easy as:

```
$ sudo pip install boto
```

With Boto installed on your client machine and an AWS EC2 interface running in front of CloudStack (see Recipe 4.1), you can now use the following script to start instances. Just replace the access and secret keys with your own and update the endpoint:

```python
#!/usr/bin/env python

import sys
import os
import boto
import boto.ec2

region = boto.ec2.regioninfo.RegionInfo(endpoint="localhost")
apikey='GwNnpUPrO6KgIdZu01z_ZhhZnKjtSdRwuYd4DvpzvFpyxGMvrzno2q05MB0ViBoFYtdqKd'
secretkey='t4eXLEYWw7chBhDlaKf38adCMSHx_wlds6JfSx3z9fSpSOm0AbP9Moj0oGIzy2LSC8iw'

def main():
    '''Establish connection to EC2 cloud'''
    conn =boto.connect_ec2(aws_access_key_id=apikey,
                           aws_secret_access_key=secretkey,
                           is_secure=False,
                           region=region,
                           port=5000,
                           path="/",
                           api_version="2014-02-01")

    '''Get list of images that I own'''
    images = conn.get_all_images()
    myimage = images[0]

        '''Pick an instance type'''
    vm_type='m1.small'
    reservation = myimage.run(instance_type=vm_type,security_groups=['default'])

if __name__ == '__main__':
    main()
```

 With Boto, you can also interact with other AWS services like S3. CloudStack has an S3 tech preview but it is backed by a standard NFS server and therefore is not a true scalable distributed block store. It will be removed from the code in an upcoming release. To provide an S3 service in your cloud, I recommend using other software like RiakCS, Ceph radosgw, or Glusterfs S3 interface. These systems handle large-scale chunking and replication.

This script will start an instance of type m1.small in a zone with security groups enabled. You could pass additional parameters to the run method like a key pair. If you are like me, you might like to have an interactive shell to your clouds, which means you might want to use Boto in a slightly different way. I use IPython (*http://ipython.org*) to get an

interactive shell, with tab completion, history, and logging capabilities. My *shell* script
is:

```python
#!/usr/bin/env python

import boto
import boto.ec2
from IPython.terminal.embed import InteractiveShellEmbed

accesskey="my api key"
secretkey="my secret key"

region = boto.ec2.regioninfo.RegionInfo(endpoint="localhost")
conn = boto.connect_ec2(aws_access_key_id=accesskey,
                        aws_secret_access_key=secretkey,
                                        is_secure=False,
                                        region=region,
                                        port=5000,
                                        path="/",
                                        api_version="2014-02-01")

ipshell = InteractiveShellEmbed(banner1="Hello, Cloud Shell!")
ipshell()
```

Starting this interactive shell, you can discover all the methods available in the
connection object by entering **conn.** and pressing the Tab key. The AWS interfaces to
CloudStack do not yet have 100% fidelity with the AWS API, so keep in mind that not
all Boto methods will work.

 In this example, I used the EC2Stack interface, but you could also use
the interface that comes natively bundled with CloudStack. Using the
packages, it can be started with service cloudstack-awsapi start.
I personally prefer EC2Stack because I was involved in the development and it supports a newer api_version.

4.5. Installing Eutester to Test the AWS Compatibility of Your CloudStack Cloud

Eutester (*https://github.com/eucalyptus/eutester*) was created by the folks at Eucalyptus
to provide a framework to create functional tests for AWS zones and Eucalyptus-based
clouds. What is interesting with *Eutester* is that it could be used to compare the AWS
compatibility of multiple clouds. Therefore, you might be wonder, "Can we use Eutester
with CloudStack?" And the answer is Yes. Certainly it could use more work, but the
basic functionality is there. It allows you to write test scenarios and compare the results
between an AWS EC2 availability zone and a CloudStack cloud.

Problem

You want to install Eutester to write integration tests for your AWS EC2 compliant cloud endpoints.

Solution

Grab the binary from the Python package index with `pip` (*https://pypi.python.org/pypi/pip*) or build it from source from GitHub.

Discussion

Install `eutester` with:

```
$ sudo pip install eutester
```

 The `master` branch of `eutester` may still cause problems to list images from a CloudStack cloud. I recently patched (*http://bit.ly/eutester_patch*) a fork of the `testing` branch and opened an issue (*http://bit.ly/eutester_issue*) on their GitHub page. You might want to check its status if you want to use Eutester heavily.

To use `eutester` with CloudStack, clone the testing branch of my Eutester fork (*https://github.com/runseb/eutester*). Then install it by hand:

```
$ git clone -b testing https://github.com/runseb/eutester.git
$ cd eutester
$ sudo python ./setup.py install
```

4.6. Using Eutester with EC2Stack to Write Functional tests

Problem

You have installed Eutester and want to write a Python script to issue requests to your CloudStack cloud.

Solution

Import the `eucaops` module in a Python script, and create a connection object using your endpoint information and your API keys. To explore your cloud interactively and create testing scenarios, use IPython.

Discussion

Start a Python/IPython interactive shell or write a script that will import ec2ops and create a connection object to your AWS EC2 compatible endpoint. For example, using EC2Stack from Recipe 4.1:

```python
#!/usr/bin/env python

from eucaops import ec2ops
from IPython.terminal.embed import InteractiveShellEmbed

accesskey="my api key"
secretkey="my secret key"

conn.ec2ops.EC2ops(endpoint="localhost",
                   aws_access_key_id=apikey,
                   aws_secret_access_key=secretkey,
                   is_secure=False,
                   port=5000,
                   path="/",
                   APIVersion="2014-02-01")

ipshell = InteractiveShellEmbed(banner1="Hello, Cloud Shell!")
ipshell()
```

Eutester, at the time of this writing, has 145 methods. Only the methods available through the CloudStack AWS EC2 interface that you will be using will be available. For example, get_zones and get_instances would return:

```
In [3]: conn.get_zones()
Out[3]: [u'ch-gva-2']

In [4]: conn.get_instances()
[2014-05-21 05:39:45,094] [EUTESTER] [DEBUG]:
--->(ec2ops.py:3164)Starting method: get_instances(self, state=None,
    idstring=None, reservation=None, rootdevtype=None, zone=None,
    key=None, pubip=None, privip=None, ramdisk=None, kernel=None,
    image_id=None, filters=None)
Out[4]:
[Instance:5a426582-3aa3-49e0-be3f-d2f9f1591f1f,
 Instance:95ee8534-b171-4f79-9e23-be48bf1a5af6,
 Instance:f18275f1-222b-455d-b352-3e7b2d3ffe9d,
 Instance:0ea66049-9399-4763-8d2f-b96e9228e413,
 Instance:7b2f63d6-66ce-4e1b-a481-e5f347f7e559,
 Instance:46d01dfd-dc81-4459-a4a8-885f05a87d07,
 Instance:7158726e-e76c-4cd4-8207-1ed50cc4d77a,
 Instance:14a0ce40-0ec7-4cf0-b908-0434271369f6]
```

This example shows that I am running eight instances at the moment in a zone called ch-gva-2, one zone of the exoscale (*http://exoscale.ch*) cloud. Selecting one of these instance objects will give you access to all the methods available for instances. You could also list, delete, and create key pairs; list, delete, and create security groups; and so on.

 Eutester is meant for building integration tests and easily creating test scenarios. If you are looking for a client to build an application with, use Boto from Recipe 4.4.

4.7. Installing and Configuring gstack: The CloudStack GCE Interface

Google Compute Engine (GCE) (*https://cloud.google.com/products/compute-engine/*) is the Google public cloud. In December 2013, Google announced the General Availability (GA) of GCE (*http://bit.ly/GA_of_GCE*). With AWS and Microsoft Azure, it is one of the three leading public clouds in the market. CloudStack has a GCE compatible interface that lets users use the GCE clients (i.e., `gcloud` and `gcutil`) to access their CloudStack cloud. Like EC2Stack, `gstack` is a Python Flask application that provides a REST API compatible with the GCE API and forwards the requests to the corresponding CloudStack API. The source is available on GitHub (*http://bit.ly/gstack*) and the binary is downloadable via PyPI (*https://pypi.python.org/pypi/gstack*).

Problem

You want to install `gstack` on your machine.

Solution

Grab the binary from the Python package index with `pip` (*https://pypi.python.org/pypi/pip*) or clone the source code from GitHub (*http://bit.ly/gstack_source*).

Discussion

You can grab the `gstack` binary package from PyPI using `pip` in one single command:

```
$ sudo pip install gstack
```

Or, if you plan to explore the source and work on it, you can Clone the repository and install it by hand:

```
$ git clone https://github.com/NOPping/gstack.git
$ sudo python ./setup.py install
```

Both of these installation methods will install a *gstack* and a *gstack-configure* binary in your path.

Before running `gstack` you must configure it. To do so, run the following:

```
$ gstack-configure
```

And enter your configuration information when prompted. You will need to specify the host and port where you want `gstack` to run on, as well as the CloudStack endpoint that you want `gstack` to forward the requests to. In the following example, we use the exoscale (*http://exoscale.ch*) cloud:

```
$ gstack-configure
gstack bind address [0.0.0.0]: localhost
gstack bind port [5000]:
Cloudstack host [localhost]: api.exoscale.ch
Cloudstack port [8080]: 443
Cloudstack protocol [http]: https
Cloudstack path [/client/api]: /compute
```

The information will be stored in a configuration file available at *~/.gstack/gstack.conf*:

```
$ cat ~/.gstack/gstack.conf
PATH = 'compute/v1/projects/'
GSTACK_BIND_ADDRESS = 'localhost'
GSTACK_PORT = '5000'
CLOUDSTACK_HOST = 'api.exoscale.ch'
CLOUDSTACK_PORT = '443'
CLOUDSTACK_PROTOCOL = 'https'
CLOUDSTACK_PATH = '/compute'
```

You can start `gstack` as easily as this:

```
$ gstack
```

Like EC2Stack, this will run `gstack` in the foreground. This is acceptable for testing purposes but if you want to run `gstack` as a service in production setup, look at some of the WSGI HTTP servers (*http://bit.ly/standalone_WSGI*) that can be used to serve `gstack`. In production, you will also need to create a properly signed certificate for `gstack` and replace the self-signed certificate.

4.8. Using gstack with the gcutil Tool

Problem

With `gstack` installed and running on your machine, you want to use the `gcutil` command-line tool to issue requests to your CloudStack cloud.

Solution

Install and configure the standalone `gcutil` tool and start issuing commands to Cloud-Stack via your running `gstack` server.

Discussion

The current version of `gstack` only works with the standalone version of `gcutil` (*http://bit.ly/standalone_gcutil*).

> Do not use the version of `gcutil` bundled in the Google Cloud SDK. Instead, install the 0.14.2 version of `gcutil`.

`gstack` comes with a self-signed certificate for the local endpoint *gstack/data/server.crt*, copy the certificate to the `gcutil` certificates file *gcutil/lib/httplib2/httplib2/cacerts.txt*.

At this stage, your CloudStack API key and secret key need to be entered in the `gcutil` *auth_helper.py* file in the *gcutil/lib/google_compute_engine/gcutil/* directory.

This is far from ideal. Thus, we opened a feature request with Google to pass the `client_id` and `client_secret` as options to `gcutil`. Hopefully a future release of `gcutil` will allow us to do so.

Create a cached parameters file for `gcutil`. Assuming you are running `gstack` on your local machine, use the defaults that were suggested during the configuration phase. Modify *~/.gcutil_params* with the following:

```
--auth_local_webserver
--auth_host_port=9999
--dump_request_response
--authorization_uri_base=https://localhost:5000/oauth2
--ssh_user=root
--fetch_discovery
--auth_host_name=localhost
--api_host=https://localhost:5000/
```

> Make sure to set the `--auth_host_name` variable to the same value as `GSTACK_BIND_ADDRESS` in your *~/.gstack/gstack.conf* file. Otherwise you will see certificates errors.

With this setup complete, gcutil will issue requests to the local Flask application, get an OAuth token, issue requests to your CloudStack endpoint, and return the response in a GCE compatible format.

With the setup steps complete, you can start issuing standard gcutil commands. For illustration purposes, we use exoscale (*http://exoscale.ch*).

 Because there are several semantic differences, you will notice that as a project, we use the account information from CloudStack. Hence, we pass our email address as the project value. This is another area that could be improved.

Let's start by listing the availability zones:

```
$ gcutil --cached_flags_file=~/.gcutil_params
         --project=runseb@gmail.com listzones
+---------+--------+------------------+
| name    | status | next-maintenance |
+---------+--------+------------------+
| ch-gva-2 | UP    | None scheduled   |
+---------+--------+------------------+
```

Let's list the machine types (or, in CloudStack terminology, the compute service offerings and the list of available images):

```
$ gcutil --cached_flags_file=~/.gcutil_params
         --project=runseb@gmail.com listmachinetypes
+-------------+----------+------+-----------+-------------+
| name        | zone     | cpus | memory-mb | deprecation |
+-------------+----------+------+-----------+-------------+
| Micro       | ch-gva-2 |   1  |    512    |             |
+-------------+----------+------+-----------+-------------+
| Tiny        | ch-gva-2 |   1  |   1024    |             |
+-------------+----------+------+-----------+-------------+
| Small       | ch-gva-2 |   2  |   2048    |             |
+-------------+----------+------+-----------+-------------+
| Medium      | ch-gva-2 |   2  |   4096    |             |
+-------------+----------+------+-----------+-------------+
| Large       | ch-gva-2 |   4  |   8182    |             |
+-------------+----------+------+-----------+-------------+
| Extra-large | ch-gva-2 |   4  |  16384    |             |
+-------------+----------+------+-----------+-------------+
| Huge        | ch-gva-2 |   8  |  32184    |             |
+-------------+----------+------+-----------+-------------+

$ ./gcutil --cached_flags_file=~/.gcutil_params
           --project=runseb@gmail.com listimages
+------------------------------------+-------------+--------+
|               name                 | deprecation | status |
+------------------------------------+-------------+--------+
```

```
| CentOS 5.5(64-bit) no GUI (KVM) |                   | Ready |
| Linux CentOS 6.4 64-bit         |                   | Ready |
| Linux CentOS 6.4 64-bit         |                   | Ready |
| Linux CentOS 6.4 64-bit         |                   | Ready |
| Linux CentOS 6.4 64-bit         |                   | Ready |
| Linux CentOS 6.4 64-bit         |                   | Ready |
| Linux Ubuntu 12.04 LTS 64-bit   |                   | Ready |
| Linux Ubuntu 12.04 LTS 64-bit   |                   | Ready |
| Linux Ubuntu 12.04 LTS 64-bit   |                   | Ready |
| Linux Ubuntu 12.04 LTS 64-bit   |                   | Ready |
| Linux Ubuntu 12.04 LTS 64-bit   |                   | Ready |
| Linux Ubuntu 13.04 64-bit       |                   | Ready |
| Linux Ubuntu 13.04 64-bit       |                   | Ready |
| Linux Ubuntu 13.04 64-bit       |                   | Ready |
| Linux Ubuntu 13.04 64-bit       |                   | Ready |
| Linux Ubuntu 13.04 64-bit       |                   | Ready |
| Windows Server 2008 R2 SP1      |                   | Ready |
| Windows Server 2008 R2 SP1      |                   | Ready |
| Windows Server 2008 R2 SP1      |                   | Ready |
| Windows Server 2008 R2 SP1      |                   | Ready |
| Windows Server 2012             |                   | Ready |
| Windows Server 2012             |                   | Ready |
| Windows Server 2012             |                   | Ready |
| Windows Server 2012             |                   | Ready |
+---------------------------------+-------------+--------+
```

You can also list firewalls, which `gstack` maps to CloudStack security groups. To create
a security group, use the firewall commands:

```
$ ./gcutil --cached_flags_file=~/.gcutil_params
        --project=runseb@gmail.com addfirewall ssh --allowed=tcp:22
```

And get the details of this firewall with `getfirewall`:

```
$ ./gcutil --cached_flags_file=~/.gcutil_params
        --project=runseb@gmail.com getfirewall ssh
+---------------+-----------+
|   property    |   value   |
+---------------+-----------+
| name          | ssh       |
| description   |           |
| creation-time |           |
| network       |           |
| source-ips    | 0.0.0.0/0 |
| source-tags   |           |
| target-tags   |           |
| allowed       | tcp: 22   |
+---------------+-----------+
```

To start an instance, you can follow the interactive prompt given by `gcutil`. You will
need to pass the `--permit_root_ssh` flag, another one of those semantic and access

configuration details that needs to be ironed out. The interactive prompt will let you choose the machine type and the image that you want; it will then start the instance:

```
$ ./gcutil --cached_flags_file=~/.gcutil_params
          --project=runseb@gmail.com addinstance foobar
Selecting the only available zone: CH-GV2
1: Extra-large  Extra-large 16384mb 4cpu
2: Huge Huge 32184mb 8cpu
3: Large     Large 8192mb 4cpu
4: Medium    Medium 4096mb 2cpu
5: Micro     Micro 512mb 1cpu
6: Small     Small 2048mb 2cpu
7: Tiny Tiny 1024mb 1cpu
7
1: CentOS 5.5(64-bit) no GUI (KVM)
2: Linux CentOS 6.4 64-bit
3: Linux CentOS 6.4 64-bit
4: Linux CentOS 6.4 64-bit
5: Linux CentOS 6.4 64-bit
6: Linux CentOS 6.4 64-bit
<...snip>
INFO: Waiting for insert of instance . Sleeping for 3s.
INFO: Waiting for insert of instance . Sleeping for 3s.

Table of resources:

+--------+--------------+--------------+----------+---------+
| name   | network-ip   | external-ip  | zone     | status  |
+--------+--------------+--------------+----------+---------+
| foobar | 185.1.2.3    | 185.1.2.3    | ch-gva-2 | RUNNING |
+--------+--------------+--------------+----------+---------+

Table of operations:

+--------------+--------+--------------------------+----------------+
| name         | status | insert-time              | operation-type |
+--------------+--------+--------------------------+----------------+
| e4180d83-31d0| DONE   | 2014-06-09T10:31:35+0200 | insert         |
+--------------+--------+--------------------------+----------------+
```

You can, of course, list (with `listinstances`) and delete instances:

```
$ ./gcutil --cached_flags_file=~/.gcutil_params --project=runseb@gmail.com
          deleteinstance foobar
Delete instance foobar? [y/n]
y
WARNING: Consider passing '--zone=CH-GV2' to avoid the unnecessary
        zone lookup which requires extra API calls.
INFO: Waiting for delete of instance . Sleeping for 3s.
+--------------+--------+--------------------------+----------------+
| name         | status | insert-time              | operation-type |
+--------------+--------+--------------------------+----------------+
```

```
| d421168c-4acd|  DONE    | 2014-06-09T10:34:53+0200 | delete        |
+--------------+--------+--------------------------+---------------+
```

gstack is still a work in progress, but it is now compatible with the GCE GA v1.0 API (*http://bit.ly/GCE_API*). The few differences in API semantics need to be investigated further and additional API calls need to be supported. However, it provides a solid base to start working on hybrid solutions between a GCE public cloud and a CloudStack-based private cloud.

4.9. Supporting the OCCI Standard in CloudStack

The Open Cloud Computing Interface (OCCI (*http://occi-wg.org*)) is a standard from the Open Grid Forum (OGF (*https://www.ogf.org/ogf/doku.php*)). OCCI was originally created to be a remote management API for the IaaS layer of cloud computing but has since evolved to also address the PaaS and SaaS layers. With CIMI (*http://dmtf.org/standards/cloud*), it is one of the two cloud standards for cloud providers' APIs backed by a standards organization. As we mentioned several times already, CloudStack has its own API, which is not a standard. AWS EC2 and Google GCE are not standards either. Cloud wrappers like libcloud and jclouds work well as unofficial standards that abstract differences in cloud providers' APIs. Users interested in using OCCI or CIMI will need a wrapper on top of the CloudStack API that will provide a CIMI or OCCI implementation. There is currently no CIMI interface for CloudStack, but through rOCCI (*https://github.com/gwdg/rOCCI-server*), there is an OCCI interface. The rest of this recipe goes through installation, configuration, and usage of the rOCCI CloudStack driver.

 There are several implementations (*http://occi-wg.org/community/implementations/*) of OCCI. rOCCI is one of them and is currently going through some refactoring.

Problem

The CloudStack API is very nice, but it is not backed by a standards organization. You care about standards and you would like to use OCCI from the Open Grid Forum to interact with your CloudStack cloud, removing any potential issues with a nonstandard API.

Solution

Install a rOCCI server in your infrastructure and configure to use the CloudStack driver. You can then use any OCCI client to issue cloud requests to it. rOCCI will forward the requests to the CloudStack API server and send the appropriate response back.

Discussion

Using OCCI with CloudStack involves running the rOCCI server and using an OCCI client to interface to it. The rOCCI server provides the API mapping between the OCCI standard API and the CloudStack API. In this discussion, the rOCCI client is used to issue OCCI API requests instead of using a CloudStack-specific client like CloudMonkey.

Install and run the rOCCI server

As we have done several times now, you can install the rOCCI server by cloning the project on GitHub (*https://github.com/gwdg/rOCCI-server*), doing a build using Ruby's bundler (*http://bundler.io*), and setting up some configuration files:

```
$ git clone https://github.com/isaacchiang/rOCCI-server.git
$ gem install bundler
$ bundle install
$ cd etc/backend
$ cp cloudstack/cloudstack.json default.json
```

The rOCCI CloudStack backend is experimental and not merged in the rOCCI server project yet.

Edit the *default.json* file to contain the information about your CloudStack cloud, your endpoint, and your API keys. Start the rOCCI server in one shell:

```
$ bundle exec passenger start
```

The server should be running on *http://0.0.0.0:3000*, and you can try to run the basic tests:

```
$ bundle exec rspec
```

You are ready to install an OCCI client and use it to talk to the rOCCI server you just started. The requests will be forwarded to your CloudStack endpoint.

Install the rOCCI client

Clone the rOCCI-cli client (*https://github.com/gwdg/rOCCI-cli*) from GitHub. Use bundler again to build it and rake to install it:

```
$ git clone https://github.com/gwdg/rOCCI-cli.git
$ cd rOCCI-cli
$ bundle install
$ bundle exec rake test
$ rake install
```

An *occi* binary should now be in your path. Try to use it by running the `--help` option:

```
$ occi --help
```

Test the OCCI client against the server

With your cloud endpoint and your API keys properly defined earlier in the *json* configuration file, you can use the OCCI client to list templates, locations, and start an instance. Similar to EC2Stack, you need to specify the endpoint of the rOCCI server that's running. Try a couple OCCI client commands:

```
$ occi --endpoint http://0.0.0.0:3000/ --action list --resource os_tpl

Os_tpl locations:
    os_tpl#6673855d-ce9b-4997-8613-6830de037a8f

$ occi --endpoint http://0.0.0.0:3000/ --action list --resource resource_tpl

Resource_tpl locations:
    resource_tpl##08ba0343-bd39-4bf0-9aab-4953694ae2b4
    resource_tpl##f78769bd-95ea-4139-ad9b-9dfc1c5cb673
    resource_tpl##0fd364a9-7e33-4375-9e10-bb861f7c6ee7
```

You will recognize the uuid from the templates and service offerings that you have created in CloudStack. These uuid will be different. To start an instance:

```
$ occi --endpoint http://0.0.0.0:3000/
        --action create
        --resource compute
        --mixin os_tpl#6673855d-ce9b-4997-8613-6830de037a8f
        --mixin resource_tpl#08ba0343-bd39-4bf0-9aab-4953694ae2b4
        --resource-title foobar
```

And voilà! The holy grail again, you started an instance on a CloudStack cloud using an OCCI client and an OCCI implementation on top of the CloudStack API.

## PART III

Configuration Management and Advanced Recipes

Making API calls either to CloudStack directly or via an API interface compatible with a public clouds API is really just the beginning. Ultimately, you want to use more advanced tools that abstract these APIs, that allow you to make use of your cloud, and that deploy applications easily and in a repeatable manner. We cover some of the well-known configuration management tools (i.e., Ansible and Chef) as well as a relatively new tool used in development (i.e., Vagrant). These tools are the foundation for automation and rapid deployments. In combination with monitoring tools, they are often associated with the DevOps (*http://devopsdays.org*) movement.

## CHAPTER 5

Configuration Management

Automation is key to a reproducible, failure-tolerant infrastructure. Cloud administrators should aim to automate all steps of building their infrastructure and be able to re-provision everything with a single click. This is possible through a combination of configuration management, monitoring, and provisioning tools. To get started in creating appliances that will be automatically configured and provisioned, three tools stand out in the arsenal: Veewee, Packer, and Vagrant.

 Veewee is being replaced by Packer (*http://www.packer.io*). There is some effort to create a CloudStack builder for Packer (*http://bit.ly/ Packer_builder*).

Vagrant (*http://vagrantup.com*) is a tool to create lightweight, portable, and reproducible development environments. Specifically, it allows you to use configuration management tools to configure a virtual machine locally (via VirtualBox) and then deploy it in the cloud via Vagrant providers. Recipe 5.4 gives you an introduction to this development tool.

A new kid on the block in configuration management and orchestration is Ansible (*http://ansibleworks.com*). Ansible is based on SSH communications with the instances and a no-server setup. It is push based at the core. It is easy to install and get started (*http://docs.ansible.com/intro.html*). Of course, just like Puppet, Salt, and Chef, it can be used in conjunction with Vagrant (*http://bit.ly/with_Vagrant*). Ansible (Recipe 5.6) has some great documentation (*http://docs.ansible.com*), so we will go quickly through the installation process and dive straight into some key concepts and a basic provisioning using Vagrant.

5.1. Installing Veewee

Problem

You need to build some virtual machine templates starting from Linux distribution ISOs. The process should be fully scripted, and reproducible. You also want to be able to do some minimal configuration, like bootstrapping a configuration management tool.

Solution

Install Veewee from GitHub.

Discussion

Veewee (*http://bit.ly/Veewee_tool*) is a tool with which you can easily create appliances for different hypervisors. It fetches the *.iso* of the distribution you want and builds the machine with a kickstart file. It integrates with providers like VirtualBox so that you can build these appliances on your local machine. It supports most commonly used OS templates. Coupled with VirtualBox, it allows admins and devs to create reproducible base appliances. Getting started with Veewee is a 10-minute exercise. The *README* is great, and there is also a very nice post (*http://bit.ly/first_box*) that guides you through your first box building.

Most folks will have no issues cloning Veewee from GitHub and building it. You will need Ruby 1.9.2 or later, which you can get via `rvm` or your favorite Ruby version manager:

```
$ git clone https://github.com/jedi4ever/veewee
$ gem install bundler
$ bundle install
```

Setting up an alias is handy at this point (e.g., `alias veewee="bundle exec veewee"`). You will need a virtual machine provider (e.g., VirtualBox, VMware Fusion, Parallels, KVM). I personally use VirtualBox, but feel free to use whichever one best suits your needs. You will then be able to start using **veewee** on your local machine.

5.2. Using Veewee to Create a Vagrant Base Box

Problem

Using Veewee, you want to create a virtual machine template from an ISO and you want to export the template for later use with Vagrant.

Solution

Select the Linux distribution that you want, define the box, configure some minimal software requirements, and build the box. To export it for use with Vagrant, use the export subcommand.

Discussion

With Veewee installed, you should be able to check all the available subcommands of veewee vbox:

```
$ veewee vbox
Commands:
  veewee vbox build [BOX_NAME]
  veewee vbox copy [BOX_NAME] [SRC] [DST]
  veewee vbox define [BOX_NAME] [TEMPLATE]
  veewee vbox destroy [BOX_NAME]
  veewee vbox export [BOX_NAME]
  veewee vbox halt [BOX_NAME]
  veewee vbox help [COMMAND]
  veewee vbox list
  veewee vbox ostypes
  veewee vbox screenshot [BOX_NAME] [PNGFILENAME]
  veewee vbox sendkeys [BOX_NAME] [SEQUENCE]
  veewee vbox ssh [BOX_NAME] [COMMAND]
  veewee vbox templates
  veewee vbox undefine [BOX_NAME]
  veewee vbox up [BOX_NAME]
  veewee vbox validate [BOX_NAME]
  veewee vbox winrm [BOX_NAME] [COMMAND]

Options:
        [--debug]            # enable debugging
  -w, --workdir, [--cwd=CWD] # Change the working directory.
```

Choose a template from the *templates* directory and define your first box. Here we call it myfirstbox, but choose your own name:

```
$ veewee vbox define myfirstbox CentOS-6.5-x86_64-minimal
```

You should see that a *defintions/* directory has been created; browse to it and inspect the *definition.rb* file. You might want to comment out some lines, like removing chef or puppet. If you don't change anything and build the box, you will then be able to validate the box with:

```
$ veewee vbox validate myfirstbox
```

To build the box, simply use the following:

```
$ veewee vbox build myfirstbox
```

If you are creating another instance of VirtualBox, you should remove the *vmwarefusion.sh* bootstrap script from the definition file. Also note that the URLs of the ISOs used by Veewee may have changed when a bug fix version was released. You might have to edit the URL in the template directory.

Everything should be successful, and you should see a running VM in your VirtualBox UI. To export it for use with Vagrant, `veewee` provides an export mechanism (really a `VBoxManage` command):

```
$ veewee vbox export myfirstbox
```

At the end of the export, a *.box* file should be present in your directory, which you can add to Vagrant with the `vagrant box add` command. The syntax will be given at the end of the Veewee `vbox export` run.

Congratulations! You have built your first Veewee box, which you can now use with Vagrant to install additional software and configure your applications.

5.3. Introducing Packer to Build Cloud Images

Packer (*http://www.packer.io*) does the same thing as Veewee but goes a step further. It helps you build base boxes in a repeatable manner, but it also integrates with configuration management systems for software provisioning on the images, and it provides a build mechanism to export images in a format suitable for various clouds and virtualization systems (e.g., AWS EC2, Google GCE, Docker). Beyond building boxes for development, it helps you build production appliances that are cloud ready. There is good documentation (*http://www.packer.io/docs*) for Packer.

Problem

As an example of using Packer, let us assume that you want to use Packer instead of Veewee to build a XenServer Vagrant box.

Solution

Use the packer-xenserver project on GitHub. It is part of a Google Summer of Code 2014 project. Clone the repository, install Packer on your machine, and build the box.

Discussion

First, you will need to install Packer. Follow the download instructions (*http://bit.ly/ Packer_install*) and you will have a *packer* binary in your path. Next, you need to clone the *packer-xenserver* repository and build the box:

```
$ git clone https://github.com/imduffy15/packer-xenserver.git
$ cd packer-xenserver
$ packer build ./template.json
```

You can look at the template file to see how the box is being configured.

If you have developed Veewee definitions file, there is a veewee-to-packer utility (*http://bit.ly/Veewee-to-Packer*) that helps you create a packer template file.

When this is done, you should see a *XenServer.box* file in the root directory. You are now ready to work with Vagrant (Recipe 5.4). Add it to your list of Vagrant boxes with:

```
$ vagrant box add xenserver ./XenServer.box
```

Create a Vagrant project with Vagrant init (in the directory of your choice) and edit the Vagrant file so that it uses the XenServer box you just added.

If you are not familiar with Vagrant yet, refer to Recipe 5.4 to get up to speed.

Disable the folder syncing functionality and the virtual box guest addition check, as it is not supported on XenServer. Define a private network as well, because host-only networks are not supported on XenServer:

```
# -*- mode: ruby -*-
# vi: set ft=ruby :

# Vagrantfile API/syntax version. Don't touch unless you know what you're doing!
VAGRANTFILE_API_VERSION = "2"

Vagrant.configure(VAGRANTFILE_API_VERSION) do |config|
  # All Vagrant configuration is done here. The most common configuration
  # options are documented and commented below. For a complete reference,
  # please see the online documentation at vagrantup.com.

  # Every Vagrant virtual environment requires a box to build off of.
  config.vm.box = "xenserver"

  config.vm.synced_folder ".", "/vagrant", disabled: true

  # disable checking for vbguest versions as its not supported on xenserver
  if Vagrant.has_plugin?("vagrant-vbguest")
    config.vbguest.auto_update = false
  end
```

```
config.vm.network :private_network, :auto_config => false ,
                                     :ip => "192.168.56.10"

config.vm.provider "virtualbox" do |v|
  v.customize ["modifyvm", :id, "--memory", 2048]
  v.customize [ "modifyvm", :id, "--nicpromisc2", "allow-all" ]
end

end
```

With this Vagrant file, you should be able to start the VM, SSH onto it, and check that
you have a Xen kernel:

```
$ vagrant up
$ vagrant ssh
Last login: Wed Jun 11 17:36:52 2014 from 10.0.2.2

XenServer dom0 configuration is tuned for maximum performance and reliability.

Configuration changes which are not explicitly documented or approved by Citrix
Technical Support, may not have been tested and are therefore not supported. In
addition, configuration changes may not persist after installation of a hotfix
or upgrade, and could also cause a hotfix or upgrade to fail.

Third party tools, which require modification to dom0 configuration, or
installation into dom0, may cease to function correctly after upgrade or hotfix
installation. Please consult Citrix Technical Support for advice regarding
specific tools.

Type "xsconsole" for access to the management console.

[vagrant@localhost ~]$ sudo su
[root@localhost vagrant]# xe vm-list
uuid ( RO)            : beb273f9-a322-4840-b861-2580fbdc67b4
    name-label ( RW): Control domain on host: localhost.localdomain
    power-state ( RO): running
```

 This box has been uploaded to the Vagrant cloud (*https://vagrant
cloud.com*), which you can get directly by referencing con
fig.vm.box = "duffy/xenserver" in your Vagrant file. This work
was done through a Google Summer of Code 2014 project.

5.4. Installing Vagrant to Build and Test Cloud Images

Problem

Building reproducible systems can be challenging. You are looking for a software development tool that allows you to test your software configuration by deploying a virtual

machine locally. You need a tool that helps you build automation and interacts with most configuration management systems used today.

Solution

Install Vagrant from binary packages downloaded on the website (*http://vagrant up.com*), add boxes that you created with Veewee (Recipe 5.1) or Packer (Recipe 5.3), and start working on your software configuration.

Discussion

To install Vagrant, you can download the latest binaries (*http://www.vagrantup.com/downloads.html*). On Ubuntu, for instance, it will be as easy as:

```
$ wget https://dl.bintray.com/mitchellh/vagrant/vagrant_1.6.2_x86_64.deb
$ dpkg -i vagrant_1.6.2_x86_64.deb
```

Vagrant will be in your path after the installation process (you can try the `vagrant --help` command to make sure it is). Picking up from where we left off with Veewee, we will add a box to Vagrant and customize it with shell scripts or much better, with Puppet recipes (*http://puppetlabs.com*), Chef cookbooks (*http://www.getchef.com*), Ansible playbooks (*http://www.ansible.com/home*), and so on. First, let's add the box (*http://bit.ly/add_box*) to Vagrant:

```
$ vagrant box add 'myfirstbox' '/path/to/box/myfirstbox.box'
```

Then in a directory of your choice, create a Vagrant project:

```
$ vagrant init 'myfirstbox'
```

This will create a Vagrant file that we will later edit to customize the box. You can boot the machine with `vagrant up` and once it's up, you can SSH to it with `vagrant ssh`.

While Veewee is used to create a base box with almost no customization (*http://bit.ly/customizing_defs*) (except potentially a Chef and/or Puppet client), Vagrant is used to customize the box using the Vagrant file. For example, to customize the `myfirstbox` that we just built, set the memory to 2 GB, add a host-only interface with IP 192.168.56.10, and finally run a *bootstrap.sh* script. We will have the following Vagrant file:

```
Vagrant.configure(VAGRANTFILE_API_VERSION) do |config|

  # Every Vagrant virtual environment requires a box to build off of.
  config.vm.box = "myfirstbox"
  config.vm.provider "virtualbox" do |vb|
    vb.customize ["modifyvm", :id, "--memory", 2048]
  end

  #host-only network setup
  config.vm.network "private_network", ip: "192.168.56.10"
```

```
#Test script to install CloudStack
config.vm.provision :shell, :path => "bootstrap.sh"
```

```
end
```

In this example, the bootstrap script should be placed in the root of the Vagrant project directory. You are now ready to dig deeper into Vagrant provisioning and get a glimpse of Vagrant's awesome power. See the provisioner documentation (*http://bit.ly/provi sioner_docs*) and pick your favorite configuration management tool. For example, with Chef (*http://www.getchef.com*), you would specify a cookbook like so:

```
config.vm.provision "chef_solo" do |chef|
    chef.add_recipe "mycookbook"
end
```

The cookbook *mycookbook* will be in a *cookbooks* directory be in the root directory of this Vagrant definition. For more information, check the Vagrant website (*http://www.vagrantup.com*) and experiment.

5.5. Using the Vagrant CloudStack Plug-In

Problem

You like testing your configurations locally, but you also want to take advantage of cloud providers. You need to use a CloudStack-based cloud to provision your virtual machines and use Vagrant to provision them with the required software.

Solution

Vagrant has a CloudStack plug-in that allows you to deploy virtual machine by sending requests to the CloudStack cloud endpoint using the API. You install the CloudStack Vagrant plug-in, define your boxes, and configure your deployments using your API keys and cloud endpoint.

Discussion

What is very interesting with Vagrant is that you can use various plug-ins to deploy machines on public clouds. There is a `vagrant-aws` plug-in to deploy on AWS and of course a `vagrant-cloudstack` plug-in. You can get the latest CloudStack plug-in from GitHub (*http://bit.ly/latest_plug-in*). You can install it directly with the `vagrant` command-line tool:

```
$ vagrant plugin install vagrant-cloudstack
```

Or if you are building it from source, clone the Git repository, build the gem, and install it in Vagrant. Replace the path used here with the one on your machine.

```
$ git clone https://github.com/klarna/vagrant-cloudstack.git
$ gem build vagrant-cloudstack.gemspec
$ gem install vagrant-cloudstack-0.1.0.gem
$ vagrant plugin install /Users/sebgoa/Documents/gitforks/ \
$ vagrant-cloudstack/vagrant-cloudstack-0.0.7.gem
```

Creating *dummy boxes* is easy to do—simply create a Vagrant file file and a *metadata.json* file like so:

```
$ cat metadata.json
{
    "provider": "cloudstack"
}
$ cat Vagrantfile
# -*- mode: ruby -*-
# vi: set ft=ruby :

Vagrant.configure("2") do |config|
  config.vm.provider :cloudstack do |cs|
    cs.template_id = "a17b40d6-83e4-4f2a-9ef0-dce6af575789"
  end
end
```

Replace the value for `cs.template_id` with a uuid of a CloudStack template in your cloud. CloudStack users will know how to easily get those `uuids` with CloudMonkey. Then create a box file with the following:

```
$ tar cvzf cloudstack.box ./metadata.json ./Vagrantfile
```

Simply add the box in Vagrant with:

```
$ vagrant box add ./cloudstack.box
```

 Remember that this is defining a local box, which references a template existing in the cloud. The only drawback to this process is that there is potential for discrepancies between the box that exists on your local machine and the template that is available in the cloud provider being used. Ideally, you would build a cloud template locally and register it in a public cloud, but this may not always be possible. In any case, you need to create dummy boxes that use existing templates available on the public cloud, as Vagrant will not register/upload a local box to the cloud on its own.

You can now create a new Vagrant project:

```
$ mkdir cloudtest
$ cd cloudtest
$ vagrant init
```

And edit the newly created Vagrant file to use the `cloudstack` box. Add additional parameters like SSH configuration, if the box does not use the default from Vagrant, plus `service_offering_id`, and so on. Remember to use your own API and secret keys and change the name of the box to what you created. For example, on exoscale (*http://www.exoscale.ch*):

```ruby
# -*- mode: ruby -*-
# vi: set ft=ruby :

# Vagrantfile API/syntax version. Don't touch unless you know what you're doing!
VAGRANTFILE_API_VERSION = "2"

Vagrant.configure(VAGRANTFILE_API_VERSION) do |config|

  # Every Vagrant virtual environment requires a box to build off of.
  config.vm.box = "cloudstack"

  config.vm.provider :cloudstack do |cs, override|
    cs.host = "api.exoscale.ch"
    cs.path = "/compute"
    cs.scheme = "https"
    cs.api_key = "PQogHs2sk_3..."
    cs.secret_key = "...NNRC5NR5cUjEg"
    cs.network_type = "Basic"

    cs.keypair = "exoscale"
    cs.service_offering_id = "71004023-bb72-4a97-b1e9-bc66dfce9470"
    cs.zone_id = "1128bd56-b4d9-4ac6-a7b9-c715b187ce11"

    override.ssh.username = "root"
    override.ssh.private_key_path = "/path/to/private/key/id_rsa_example"
  end

  # Test bootstrap script
  config.vm.provision :shell, :path => "bootstrap.sh"

end
```

The machine is brought up with:

```
$ vagrant up --provider=cloudstack
```

The following example output will follow:

```
$ vagrant up --provider=cloudstack
Bringing machine 'default' up with 'cloudstack' provider...
[default] Warning! The Cloudstack provider doesn't support any of the Vagrant
high-level network configurations (`config.vm.network`). They
will be silently ignored.
[default] Launching an instance with the following settings...
[default]  -- Service offering UUID: 71004023-bb72-4a97-b1e9-bc66dfce9470
[default]  -- Template UUID: a17b40d6-83e4-4f2a-9ef0-dce6af575789
[default]  -- Zone UUID: 1128bd56-b4d9-4ac6-a7b9-c715b187ce11
[default]  -- Keypair: exoscale
[default] Waiting for instance to become "ready"...
```

```
[default] Waiting for SSH to become available...
[default] Machine is booted and ready for use!
[default] Rsyncing folder: /Users/sebgoa/Documents/exovagrant/ => /vagrant
[default] Running provisioner: shell...
[default] Running: /var/folders/76/sx82k6cd6cxbp7_djngd17f80000gn/T
                   /vagrant-shell20131203-21441-1ipxq9e
Tue Dec  3 14:25:49 CET 2013
This works
```

Which is a perfect execution of my amazing bootstrap script:

```
#!/usr/bin/env bash

/bin/date
echo "This works"
```

You can now start playing with Chef cookbooks, Puppet recipes, and Ansible playbooks, and automate the configuration of your cloud instances.

> I would be remiss if I did not mention a nice feature of Vagrant. It can handle multiple machine definitions. This means that in a single Vagrant file you can define different instances, boot them, and provision them in parallel (*http://bit.ly/multi-machine*):
>
> ```
> config.vm.define "web" do |web|
>   web.vm.box = "tutorial"
> end
>
> config.vm.define "db" do |db|
>   db.vm.box = "tutorial"
> end
> ```
>
> You can control each machine separately (i.e., vagrant up web and vagrant up db) or all at once in parallel (i.e., vagrant up).

Let the fun begin. Pick your favorite configuration management tool, decide what you want to provision, set up your recipes, and launch the instances.

5.6. Introducing Ansible to Configure Cloud Instances

Problem

You are looking for a configuration management system that can also perform remote execution and complex application deployments that some people refer to as orchestration (*http://bit.ly/complex_deployments*). In addition, you are more familiar with Python than Ruby.

Solution

Use Ansible (*http://www.ansibleworks.com*). Download the binary package via the Python Package Index and you are ready to go.

Discussion

First, install `ansible`:

```
$ pip install ansible
```

Or get it via packages `yum install ansible`, `apt-get install ansible` if you have set the proper repositories (*http://bit.ly/Ansible_install*).

Let's say you have two instances running and SSH access to them. Create an inventory *inv* file with the IP addresses of the instances. For example:

```
185.1.2.3
185.3.4.5
```

Then run `ping`, your first Ansible command:

```
$ ansible all -i inv -m ping
```

You should see the following output:

```
185.1.2.3 | success >> {
    "changed": false,
    "ping": "pong"
}

185.3.4.5 | success >> {
    "changed": false,
    "ping": "pong"
}
```

And see how you can use Ansible as a remote execution framework:

```
$ ansible all -i inv -a "/bin/echo hello"
185.1.2.3 | success | rc=0 >>
hello

185.3.4.5 | success | rc=0 >>
hello
```

You should get the feel that Ansible is more than pure configuration management as it can do remote execution, much like Salt or some old school multithreaded SSH execution framework.

5.7. Provisioning with Ansible Playbooks

Problem

With Ansible installed, you want to use some existing configuration recipes to install software on some remote systems. You also want to use it with Vagrant to test your recipes locally, then deploy them on remote instances in the cloud.

Solution

Use the `ansible-playbook` command to execute a set of configuration tasks called plays (hence the term playbook). You will need an inventory of machine and potentially some additional options like SSH key pairs. Conveniently, Vagrant supports Ansible provisioning natively. You can specify the playbooks you want to use when deploying a machine with Vagrant as well as pass optional arguments to the deployment.

Discussion

Now check some of the Ansible examples (*https://github.com/ansible/ansible-examples*) available on GitHub. We are going to walk through the WordPress example. Clone the entire project, go to the WordPress example, and create an inventory file:

```
$ git clone https://github.com/ansible/ansible-examples.git
$ cd ansible-examples/wordpress-nginx
```

If you check the *README.md* file, it will tell you how to create the inventory. Create a *hosts* file and add the IP addresses of the instances you had running in Recipe 5.6. Now you can use the `ansible-playbook` command to start configuring the instances. If you are using a special SSH key, then specify it with the `--private-key` option:

```
$ cp hosts.example hosts
$ vi hosts
$ ansible-playbook -i hosts --private-key=~/.ssh/id_rsa site.yml
```

Ansible will configure the machines and you will end up with two working WordPress sites.

The previous example assumed some running instances (e.g., local VMs or in the cloud). In this recipe, we are going to use Vagrant, but instead of using a shell or a puppet provisioner, we are going to use the Ansible provisioner.

Go back to the Vagrant project directory we have been working on and edit the Vagrant file. Remove the Puppet provisioning (or comment it out) and add:

```
# Ansible test
config.vm.provision "ansible" do |ansible|
  ansible.playbook = "ansible/site.yml"
  ansible.verbose = "vvvv"
```

```
      ansible.host_key_checking = "false"
      ansible.sudo_user = "root"
      ansible.raw_arguments = "-s"
    end
```

The *site.yml* playbook referenced needs to be located in the *ansible* subdirectory. You can get the WordPress playbook that we used in Recipe 5.6. Clone the Ansible examples repository, and copy the WordPress playbook in the *ansible* directory, for example:

```
mkdir ansible
cd ansible
git clone https://github.com/ansible/ansible-examples.git
cd ansible-examples/wordpress-nginx
cp -R * ../../
```

The complete Vagrant file will look like this:

```
# -*- mode: ruby -*-
# vi: set ft=ruby :

# Vagrantfile API/syntax version. Don't touch unless you know what you're doing!
VAGRANTFILE_API_VERSION = "2"

Vagrant.configure(VAGRANTFILE_API_VERSION) do |config|

  config.vm.box = "centos64"
  config.vm.provider "virtualbox" do |vb|
    vb.customize ["modifyvm", :id, "--memory", 2048]
    vb.customize ["modifyvm", :id, "--nicpromisc2", "allow-all"]
  end

  config.vm.provision "ansible" do |ansible|
    ansible.playbook = "ansible/site.yml"
    ansible.inventory_path = "ansible/hosts"
    ansible.extra_vars = { ansible_ssh_user: 'vagrant'}
    ansible.verbose = "vvvv"
    ansible.host_key_checking = "false"
    ansible.sudo_user = "root"
    ansible.sudo = "True"
    ansible.raw_arguments = "-s"
  end

  # Bridge networking
  config.vm.network "private_network", ip: "192.168.50.110"

end
```

And start the instance once again:

```
$ vagrant up
```

Watch the output from the Ansible provisioning and, once finished, access the WordPress application that was just configured.

You might have to edit the playbook. I removed the `selinux` task in the MySQL setup (*http://bit.ly/MySQL_setup*).

With a Vagrant VM set up and Ansible installed locally, you can always run the playbook manually with:

```
$ ansible-playbook -i hosts -s -u vagrant \
    --private-key=/Users/sebgoa/.vagrant.d/insecure_private_key site.yml
```

Just replace the path of the Vagrant SSH key being used.

5.8. Ansible Provisioning with Vagrant CloudStack Plug-In

Problem

Mastering Ansible on a local test machine is very handy, but you are looking for more. You want to use it to automatically configure cloud instances.

Solution

Vagrant comes with a CloudStack plug-in that can be used in combination with Ansible. Vagrant will start the machine in your CloudStack cloud and then use Ansible with the right options to apply the playbooks. In addition, Ansible comes with a dynamic inventory script based on libcloud (Recipe 3.7) that will allow you to poll the CloudStack endpoint, retrieve information about running instances, and build an inventory file compatible with Ansible for later use.

Discussion

Provisioning locally in a VirtualBox VM is great, but we also want to be able to do the same remotely and provision an instance in the cloud.

The only thing we need to do is to use the CloudStack plug-in in Vagrant, and update the Vagrant file to contain API keys and a few pieces of information that your CloudStack endpoint needs to start the instance. Here is a fully working example:

```
VAGRANTFILE_API_VERSION = "2"

Vagrant.configure(VAGRANTFILE_API_VERSION) do |config|

  config.vm.box ="centos-cloud"
  config.vm.host_name ="webserver"

  config.ssh.username = "root"
```

```
config.ssh.private_key_path = "/Users/sebgoa/.ssh/id_rsa_oreilly"
config.ssh.pty = "true"

config.vm.provider :cloudstack do |cloudstack, override|
    cloudstack.api_key = ""
    cloudstack.secret_key = ""
    cloudstack.service_offering_id = "71004023-bb72-4a97-b1e9-bc66dfce9470"
    cloudstack.keypair = "oreilly" # SSH Key pair to access machine
end

config.vm.provision "ansible" do |ansible|
  ansible.playbook = "ansible/site.yml"
  ansible.groups = {"wordpress-server" => ["default"]}
  ansible.verbose = "vvvv"
  ansible.host_key_checking = "false"
  ansible.sudo_user = "root"
  ansible.sudo = "True"
  ansible.raw_arguments = "-s"
end

end
```

You will notice several things. We defined a `config.ssh.username` and a `con`
`fig.ssh.private_key_path`, which are used by Vagrant to SSH to the instance. We also
set `config.ssh.pty` to `True` to allow sudo commands over SSH on CentOS. The Cloud-
Stack provider information will need your API and secret keys as well as the *service
offering* of the instance (e.g., two cores, 2 GB RAM) and if you are using SSH key pair
access, you will need to define that key pair.

The Ansible provisioning section is almost the same as with the local provisioning
example in Recipe 5.7. We only added a `ansible.groups` variable to make use of the
fact that Vagrant creates an Ansible inventory on the fly (*http://docs.ansible.com/
guide_vagrant.html*).

With this Vagrant file created, you can start the instance in your favorite CloudStack
cloud. When Ansible finishes, open your browser at the IP of your instance on port 80
and you will see a brand new WordPress site.

```
$ vagrant up --provider=cloudstack
```

Finally, Ansible features a set of scripts (*http://bit.ly/Ansible_scripts*) used to create an
inventory (*http://bit.ly/dynamic_inventory*) of instances, grouped by properties. The
`apache-libcloud` script can be used to poll a CloudStack cloud for its inventory of
machines.

Get the script (*http://bit.ly/inventory_script*) and the configuration (*http://bit.ly/
config_file*) file or clone the Ansible repo and go to the *plugins/inventory* directory:

```
$ git clone https://github.com/ansible/ansible.git
$ cd plugins/inventory
```

Edit the configuration file (*libcloud.ini*) to point to your CloudStack endpoint and add your API keys. The following example uses exoscale and sets the path to the inventory cache to */home/sebgoa*:

```
# Ansible Apache Libcloud Generic inventory script

[driver]
provider = CLOUDSTACK
host = api.exoscale.ch
path = /compute
secure = True
verify_ssl_cert = True

key =
secret =

[cache]
cache_path=
cache_max_age=60
```

With this configuration set, you can generate an inventory with the following:

```
python ./apache-libcloud.py
{
  "0ea66049-9399-4763-8d2f-b96e9228e413": [
    "185.1.2.3"
  ],
  "80e7fc8e-0bd8-4c4d-9857-43dadbe95847": [
    "185.1.2.4"
  ],
  "key_foobar": [
    "185.1.2.3",
    "185.1.2.4"
  ],
  "sg_default": [
    "185.1.2.4"
  ],
  "sg_foobar": [
    "185.1.2.3"
  ]
}
```

You can work with all the instances in your cloud using this script (to learn more, check the Ansible dynamic inventory documentation (*http://bit.ly/dynamic_inventory*)):

```
$ ansible all -i ./apache-libcloud.py --private-key=~/.ssh/id_rsa_exoscale \
> -m ping
```

5.9. Installing knife-cloudstack

Problem

Knife is a command-line utility for Chef, the configuration management system from OpsCode. You use Chef and want to use Knife with your CloudStack cloud.

Solution

The Knife family of tools are drivers that automate the provisioning and configuration of machines in the Cloud. `knife-cloudstack` is a CloudStack plug-in for Knife. Written in Ruby, it is used by the Chef community.

Discussion

To install `knife-cloudstack`, you can simply install the gem or get it from GitHub:

```
$ sudo gem install knife-cloudstack
```

If successful, the `knife` command should now be in your path. Issue `knife` at the prompt and see the various options and subcommands available.

If you want to use the version on GitHub simply clone it:

```
$ git clone https://github.com/CloudStack-extras/knife-cloudstack.git
```

If you clone the Git repo and make changes to the code, you will want to build and install a new gem. As an example, in the directory where you cloned the *knife-cloudstack* repo do the following:

```
$ gem build knife-cloudstack.gemspec
  Successfully built RubyGem
  Name: knife-cloudstack
  Version: 0.0.14
  File: knife-cloudstack-0.0.14.gem
$ gem install knife-cloudstack-0.0.14.gem
  Successfully installed knife-cloudstack-0.0.14
  1 gem installed
  Installing ri documentation for knife-cloudstack-0.0.14...
  Installing RDoc documentation for knife-cloudstack-0.0.14...
```

You will then need to define your CloudStack endpoint and your credentials in a *knife.rb* file like so:

```
knife[:cloudstack_url] = "http://yourcloudstackserver.com:8080/client/api"
knife[:cloudstack_api_key]  = "Your CloudStack API Key"
knife[:cloudstack_secret_key] = "Your CloudStack Secret Key"
```

With the endpoint and credentials configured as well as `knife-cloudstack` installed, you should be able to issue your first command. Remember that this is simply sending

---

a CloudStack API call to your CloudStack-based cloud provider. Later in the recipe, we will see how to do more advanced things with `knife-cloudstack`. For example, to list the service offerings (i.e., instance types) available on the iKoula Cloud, do this:

```
$ knife cs service list
Name            Memory  CPUs  CPU Speed  Created
m1.extralarge   15GB    8     2000 Mhz   2013-05-27T16:00:11+0200
m1.large        8GB     4     2000 Mhz   2013-05-27T15:59:30+0200
m1.medium       4GB     2     2000 Mhz   2013-05-27T15:57:46+0200
m1.small        2GB     1     2000 Mhz   2013-05-27T15:56:49+0200
```

To list all the `knife-cloudstack` commands available just enter `knife cs` at the prompt. You will see:

```
$ knife cs
Available cs subcommands: (for details, knife SUB-COMMAND --help)

** CS COMMANDS **
knife cs account list (options)
knife cs cluster list (options)
knife cs config list (options)
knife cs disk list (options)
knife cs domain list (options)
knife cs firewallrule list (options)
knife cs host list (options)
knife cs hosts
knife cs iso list (options)
knife cs template create NAME (options)
...
```

 If you only have user privileges on the cloud you are using, as opposed to admin privileges, do note that some commands won't be available to you. For instance, on the cloud I am using where I am a standard user, I cannot access any of the infrastructure type commands like:

```
$ knife cs pod list
Error 432: Your account does not have the right to execute
           his command or the command does not exist.
```

Similar to CloudMonkey, you can pass a list of fields to output. To find the potential fields, include the `--fieldlist` option at the end of the command. You can then pick the fields that you want to output by passing a comma-separated list to the `--fields` option like so:

```
$ knife cs service list --fieldlist
Name            Memory  CPUs  CPU Speed  Created
m1.extralarge   15GB    8     2000 Mhz   2013-05-27T16:00:11+0200
m1.large        8GB     4     2000 Mhz   2013-05-27T15:59:30+0200
m1.medium       4GB     2     2000 Mhz   2013-05-27T15:57:46+0200
m1.small        2GB     1     2000 Mhz   2013-05-27T15:56:49+0200
```

```
Key          Type         Value
cpunumber    Fixnum       8
cpuspeed     Fixnum       2000
created      String       2013-05-27T16:00:11+0200
defaultuse   FalseClass   false
displaytext  String       8 Cores CPU with 15.3GB RAM
domain       String       ROOT
domainid     String       1
hosttags     String       ex10
id           String       1412009f-0e89-4cfc-a681-1cda0631094b
issystem     FalseClass   false
limitcpuuse  TrueClass    true
memory       Fixnum       15360
name         String       m1.extralarge
networkrate  Fixnum       100
offerha      FalseClass   false
storagetype  String       local
tags         String       ex10

$ knife cs service list --fields id,name,memory,cpunumber
id                                     name           memory  cpunumber
1412009f-0e89-4cfc-a681-1cda0631094b   m1.extralarge  15360   8
d2b2e7b9-4ffa-419e-9ef1-6d413f08deab   m1.large       7680    4
8dae8be9-5dae-4f81-89d1-b171f25ef3fd   m1.medium      3840    2
c6b89fea-1242-4f54-b15e-9d8ec8a0b7e8   m1.small       1740    1
```

5.10. Starting an Instance with Knife

Problem

You want to start an instance in the cloud using Knife and you'd like to configure it with some recipes using Chef.

Solution

In order to manage instances, Knife has several commands:

- `knife cs server list` to list all instances
- `knife cs server start` to restart a paused instance
- `knife cs server stop` to suspend a running instance
- `knife cs server delete` to destroy an instance
- `knife cs server reboot` to reboot a running instance

And of course to create an instance, use `knife cs server create`.

Discussion

Knife will automatically allocate a public IP address and associate it with your running instance. If you additionally pass some port forwarding rules and firewall rules, it will set those up. You need to specify an instance type, from the list returned by `knife cs service list`, as well as a template, from the list returned by `knife cs template list`. The `--no-boostrap` option will tell Knife not to install Chef on the deployed instance. Syntax for the port forwarding and firewall rules are explained on the Knife CloudStack (*http://bit.ly/Knife_CloudStack*) website. Here is an example on the iKoula cloud (*http://www.ikoula.com*) in France:

```
$ knife cs server create --no-bootstrap --service m1.small
                     --template "CentOS 6.4 - Minimal - 64bits" foobar

Waiting for Server to be created.......
Allocate ip address, create forwarding rules
params: {"command"=>"associateIpAddress",
        "zoneId"=>"a41b82a0-78d8-4a8f-bb79-303a791bb8a7",
        "networkId"=>"df2288bb-26d7-4b2f-bf41-e0fae1c6d198"}.
Allocated IP Address: 178.170.XX.XX
...
Name:      foobar
Public IP:  178.170.XX.XX

$ knife cs server list
Name    Public IP        Service    Template    State    Instance  Hypervisor
foobar  178.170.XX.XX    m1.small   CentOS 6.4  Running  N/A       N/A
```

5.11. Bootstrapping Instances with Hosted Chef

Problem

You want to use Knife with Hosted Chef

Solution

Knife lives up to its full potential when used to bootstrap Chef and use it for configuration management of the instances. The easiest way to get started with Chef is to use Hosted Chef (*https://manage.opscode.com/signup*). There is some great documentation on how (*http://learn.getchef.com/legacy/get-started/*) to do it. The basic concept is that you will download or create cookbooks locally and publish them to your own hosted Chef server.

Discussion

With your *hosted Chef* account created and your local *chef-repo* setup, you can start instances on your Cloud and specify the cookbooks to use to configure those instances.

The bootstrapping process will fetch those cookbooks and configure the node. Here is an example that does so using the exoscale (*http://www.exoscale.ch*) cloud, which runs on CloudStack. This cloud is enabled as a basic zone and uses SSH key pairs and security groups for access:

```
$ knife cs server create --service Tiny --template "Linux CentOS 6.4 64-bit"
  --ssh-user root --identity ~/.ssh/id_rsa --run-list "recipe[apache2]"
  --ssh-keypair foobar --security-group www --no-public-ip foobar

Waiting for Server to be created....
Name:        foobar
Public IP:   185.19.XX.XX


Waiting for sshd.....

Name:          foobar13
Public IP:     185.19.XX.XX
Environment:   _default
Run List:      recipe[apache2]

Bootstrapping Chef on 185.19.XX.XX
185.19.XX.XX  --2013-06-10 11:47:54--  http://opscode.com/chef/install.sh
185.19.XX.XX  Resolving opscode.com...
185.19.XX.XX  184.ZZ.YY.YY
185.19.XX.XX Connecting to opscode.com|184.ZZ.XX.XX|:80...
185.19.XX.XX connected.
185.19.XX.XX HTTP request sent, awaiting response...
185.19.XX.XX 301 Moved Permanently
185.19.XX.XX Location: http://www.opscode.com/chef/install.sh [following]
185.19.XX.XX --2013-06-10 11:47:55--  http://www.opscode.com/chef/install.sh
185.19.XX.XX Resolving www.opscode.com...
185.19.XX.XX 184.ZZ.YY.YY
185.19.XX.XX Reusing existing connection to opscode.com:80.
185.19.XX.XX HTTP request sent, awaiting response...
185.19.XX.XX 200 OK
185.19.XX.XX Length: 6509 (6.4K) [application/x-sh]
185.19.XX.XX Saving to: "STDOUT"
185.19.XX.XX
 0% [                                      ] 0          ---.-K/s
100%[=====================================>] 6,509      ---.-K/s   in 0.1s
185.19.XX.XX
185.19.XX.XX 2013-06-10 11:47:55 (60.8 KB/s) - written to stdout [6509/6509]
185.19.XX.XX
185.19.XX.XX Downloading Chef 11.4.4 for el...
185.19.XX.XX Installing Chef 11.4.4
```

Chef will then configure the machine based on the cookbook passed in the `--run-list` option; here I set up a simple web server. Note the key pair that I used and the security group. I also specify `--no-public-ip`, which disables the IP address allocation and association. This is specific to the setup of *exoscale*, which automatically uses a public IP address for the instances.

 The latest version of `knife-cloudstack` allows you to manage key pairs and security groups. For example, listing, creating, and deleting of key pairs is possible, as well as listing of security groups:

```
$ knife cs securitygroup list
Name      Description                  Account
default   Default Security Group       runseb@gmail.com
www       apache server                runseb@gmail.com
$ knife cs keypair list
Name       Fingerprint
exoscale   xx:xx:xx:xx:xx:xx:xx:xx:xx:xx:xx:xx:xx:xx:xx:xx
```

When using a CloudStack-based cloud in an advanced zone setting, Knife can automatically allocate and associate an IP address. To illustrate this slightly different example, I use iKoula (*http://www.ikoula.com*), a French cloud provider that uses CloudStack. I edit my *knife.rb* file to set up a different endpoint and the different API and secret keys. I remove the key pair, security group, and public IP option, and I do not specify an identity file, as I will retrieve the SSH password with the `--cloudstack-password` option. The example is as follows:

```
$ knife cs server create --service m1.small
  --template "CentOS 6.4 - Minimal - 64bits"
  --ssh-user root --cloudstack-password --run-list "recipe[apache2]" foobar

Waiting for Server to be created.......
Allocate ip address, create forwarding rules
params: {"command"=>"associateIpAddress",
        "zoneId"=>"a41b82a0-78d8-4a8f-bb79-303a791bb8a7",
        "networkId"=>"df2288bb-26d7-4b2f-bf41-e0fae1c6d198"}.
Allocated IP Address: 178.170.71.148
...
Name:      foobar
Password:  $%@#$%#$%#$
Public IP: 178.xx.yy.zz


Waiting for sshd......

Name:        foobar
Public IP:   178.xx.yy.zz
Environment: _default
Run List:    recipe[apache2]

Bootstrapping Chef on 178.xx.yy.zz
178.xx.yy.zz --2013-06-10 13:24:29--  http://opscode.com/chef/install.sh
178.xx.yy.zz Resolving opscode.com...
```

You will want to review the security implications of doing the bootstrap as root and using the default password to do so.

In advanced zone, your cloud provider may also have decided to block all egress traffic to the public Internet, which means that contacting the hosted Chef server would fail. To configure the egress rules properly, CloudMonkey can be used. List the networks to find the ID of your guest network, then create an egress firewall rule. Review the Cloud-Monkey recipe (Recipe 3.3) to find the proper API calls and their arguments:

```
> list networks filter=id,name,netmask
count = 1
network:
+-----------------------------------+------+---------------+
|                id                 | name |    netmask    |
+-----------------------------------+------+---------------+
| df2288bb-26d7-4b2f-bf41-e0fae1c6d198 | test | 255.255.255.0 |
+-----------------------------------+------+---------------+

> create egressfirewallrule networkid=df2288bb-26d7-4b2f-bf41-e0fae1c6d198
        startport=80 endport=80 protocol=TCP cidrlist=10.1.1.0/24
id = b775f1cb-a0b3-4977-90b0-643b01198367
jobid = 8a5b735c-6aab-45f8-b687-0a1150a66e0f

> list egressfirewallrules filter=networkid,startport,endport,cidrlist,protocol
count = 1
firewallrule:
+-----------+---------+-------------+--------+----------+
| startport | endport |  cidrlist   | state  | protocol |
+-----------+---------+-------------+--------+----------+
|    80     |   80    | 10.1.1.0/24 | Active |   tcp    |
+-----------+---------+-------------+--------+----------+
```

## CHAPTER 6

Advanced Recipes

In this final chapter, we cover some advanced tools and use cases focused on application deployments and enhancement to your cloud infrastructure. Fluent is a log aggregation framework that you can use in your monitoring environment to store and analyze your logs. In combination with MongoDB or Elasticsearch, it is a very powerful tool. RiakCS is a scalable distributed object store created by Basho and provides an S3-compatible API. Together with a tool like EC2Stack, it can help you build an EC2/S3 clone. Apache Whirr is an automation tool to create clusters of virtual machines that form complete distributed systems, and in theses recipes, we'll use Whirr to provision a Hadoop cluster. This final chapter rounds up the ecosystem, going from installation, clients, wrappers, configuration management, and software development tools to application deployment, monitoring, and high lever services to your cloud.

6.1. Installing Fluentd to Collect CloudStack Logs and Events

Fluentd (*http://fluentd.org*) is an open source software to collect events and logs in JSON format. It has hundreds of plug-ins that allow you to store the logs/events in your favorite data store like AWS S3, MongoDB, and even Elasticsearch. It is an equivalent to log stash (*http://logstash.net*). The source is available on GitHub (*https://github.com/fluent/fluentd*), but can also be installed via your favorite package manager (e.g., brew, yum, apt, gem). A CloudStack plug-in listens to CloudStack events and stores these events in a chosen storage backend. In this chapter, we will show how to store CloudStack logs in Elasticsearch using Fluent. Note that the same thing can be done with logstash. The documentation (*http://docs.fluentd.org/articles/quickstart*) is quite straightforward, but here are the basic steps.

Problem

You want to use Fluent to aggregate logs from various systems in your data center.

Solution

Install a Fluent Ruby gem, generate a configuration file, and start the `fluentd` plug-in.

Discussion

You will need a working `fluentd` installed on your machine. Pick your package manager of choice and install `fluentd`. For instance, with `gem` we would do:

```
$ sudo gem install fluentd
```

`fluentd` will now be in your path. You need to create a configuration file and start `fluentd` using this config. For additional options with `fluentd`, just enter `fluentd -h`. The `-s` option will create a sample configuration file in the working directory. The `-c` option will start `fluentd` using the specific configuration file. You can then send a test log/event message to the running process with `fluent-cat`:

```
$ fluentd -s conf
$ fluentd -c conf/fluent.conf &
$ echo '{"json":"message"}' | fluent-cat debug.test
```

6.2. Configuring the CloudStack Fluentd Plug-In

Problem

CloudStack has a `listEvents` API that does exactly what its name suggests: it lists events happening within a CloudStack deployment. For example, it can list events such as the start and stop of a virtual machine, creation of security groups, life cycle events of storage elements, snapshots, and more.

Solution

The `listEvents` API is well documented (*http://bit.ly/listEvents_API*). Based mostly on this API and the Fog (*http://fog.io*) Ruby library, a CloudStack plug-in for `fluentd` was written by Yuichi UEMURA (*https://github.com/u-ichi*). It is slightly different from using `logstash`, as with `logstash` you can format the log4j logs of the CloudStack management server and directly collect those. Here we rely on the `listEvents` API.

Discussion

You can install the plug-in from source via GitHub:

```
$ git clone https://github.com/u-ichi/fluent-plugin-cloudstack
```

Then build your own gem and install it with the following:

```
$ sudo gem build fluent-plugin-cloudstack.gemspec
$ sudo gem install fluent-plugin-cloudstack-0.0.8.gem
```

Or install the gem directly:

```
$ sudo gem install fluent-plugin-cloudstack
```

You will need to generate a configuration file with `fluentd -s conf`. You can specify the path to your configuration file. Edit the configuraton to define a `source` as being from your CloudStack host. For instance, if you are running a development environment locally:

```
<source>
  type cloudstack
  host localhost
  apikey $cloudstack_apikey
  secretkey $cloustack_secretkey

  # optional
  protocol http          # https or http, default https
  path /client/api       # default /client/api
  port 8080              # default 443
  interval 300           # min 300, default 300
  ssl false              # true or false, default true
  domain_id $cloudstack_domain_id
  tag cloudstack
</source>
```

You also want to define the tag explicitly as being `cloudstack`. You can then create a `<match>` section in the configuration file. To keep it simple at first, we will echo the events to `stdout`. Just add the following:

```
<match cloudstack.**>
  type stdout
</match>
```

Run `fluentd` with `fluentd -c conf/fluent.conf &`, browse the CloudStack UI, create a VM, and create a service offering. Once the interval is passed, you will see the events being written to `stdout`:

```
2013-11-05 12:19:26 +0100 [info]: starting fluentd-0.10.39
2013-11-05 12:19:26 +0100 [info]: reading config file path="conf/fluent.conf"
2013-11-05 12:19:26 +0100 [info]: using configuration file: <ROOT>
  <source>
    type forward
  </source>
  <source>
    type cloudstack
    host localhost
```

```
apikey 6QN8jOzEfhR7Fua69vk5ocDo_tfg8qqkT7-
secretkey HZiu9vhPAxA8xi8jpGWMWb9q9f5OL1ojW4
protocol http
path /client/api
port 8080
interval 3
ssl false
domain_id a9e4b8f0-3fd5-11e3-9df7-78ca8b5a2197
tag cloudstack
</source>
<match debug.**>
  type stdout
</match>
<match cloudstack.**>
  type stdout
</match>
</ROOT>
2013-11-05 12:19:26 +0100 [info]: adding source type="forward"
2013-11-05 12:19:26 +0100 [info]: adding source type="cloudstack"
2013-11-05 12:19:27 +0100 [info]: adding match pattern="debug.**" type="stdout"
2013-11-05 12:19:27 +0100 [info]: adding match pattern="cloudstack.**"
                                  type="stdout"
2013-11-05 12:19:27 +0100 [info]: listening fluent socket on 0.0.0.0:24224
2013-11-05 12:19:27 +0100 [info]: listening cloudstack api on localhost
2013-11-05 12:19:30 +0100 cloudstack.usages: {"events_flow":0}
2013-11-05 12:19:30 +0100 cloudstack.usages:
{"vm_sum":1,"memory_sum":536870912,"cpu_sum":1,"root_volume_sum":1400,
 "data_volume_sum":0,"Small Instance":1}
2013-11-05 12:19:33 +0100 cloudstack.usages: {"events_flow":0}
2013-11-05 12:19:33 +0100 cloudstack.usages:
{"vm_sum":1,"memory_sum":536870912,"cpu_sum":1,"root_volume_sum":1400,
 "data_volume_sum":0,"Small Instance":1}
2013-11-05 12:19:36 +0100 cloudstack.usages: {"events_flow":0}
2013-11-05 12:19:36 +0100 cloudstack.usages:
{"vm_sum":1,"memory_sum":536870912,"cpu_sum":1,"root_volume_sum":1400,
 "data_volume_sum":0,"Small Instance":1}
2013-11-05 12:19:39 +0100 cloudstack.usages: {"events_flow":0}
...
```

I cut some of the output for brevity. Note that I do have an interval listed as 3 because I did not want to wait 300 minutes. Therefore, I installed from source and patched the plug-in; it should be fixed in the source soon. You might have a different endpoint and of course different keys, and don't worry about me sharing that secret_key (I am using a simulator, and that key is already gone).

6.3. Using MongoDB as a Fluent Data Store

Problem

Getting the events and usage information on stdout is interesting, but the most interesting part comes when you want to store the data in a database or a search index.

Solution

Use the MongoDB (*http://www.mongodb.org*) NoSQL document store, to keep an archive of CloudStack events aggregated by Fluent. Perform queries on your CloudStack logs using MongoDB.

Discussion

MongoDB is an open source document database that is schemaless and stores documents in JSON format (BSON actually). Installation and query syntax of MongoDB is beyond the scope of this chapter. MongoDB clusters can be set up with replication and sharding. In this recipe, we use MongoDB on a single host with no sharding or replication. To use MongoDB as a storage backend for the events, we first need to install MongoDB. On a single OS X node, this is as simple as sudo port install mongodb. For other operating systems, use the appropriate package manager. You can then start MongoDB with sudo mongod --dbpath=/path/to/your/databases. Create a flu entd database and a fluentd user with read/write access to it. In the Mongo shell do the following:

```
$ sudo mongo
>use fluentd
>db.AddUser({user:"fluentd", pwd: "foobar", roles: ["readWrite", "dbAdmin"]})
```

We then need to install the fluent-plugin-mongodb. Still using gem, this will be done like so:

```
$ sudo gem install fluent-plugin-mongo
```

The complete documentation (*http://docs.fluentd.org/articles/out_mongo*) also explains how to modify the configuration of fluentd to use this backend. Previously, we used stdout as the output backend. To use MongoDB, we just need to write a different <match> section like so:

```
# Single MongoDB
<match cloudstack.**>
  type mongo
  host fluentd
  port 27017
  database fluentd
  collection test
```

```
  # for capped collection
  capped
  capped_size 1024m

  # authentication
  user fluentd
  password foobar

  # flush
  flush_interval 10s
</match>
```

Note that you cannot have multiple `match` sections for the same tag pattern.

To view the events/usages in Mongo, simply start a Mongo shell with `mongo -u fluentd -p foobar fluentd` and list the collections. You will see the `test` collection:

```
$ mongo -u fluentd -p foobar fluentd
MongoDB shell version: 2.4.7
connecting to: fluentd
Server has startup warnings:
Fri Nov  1 13:11:44.855 [initandlisten]
Fri Nov  1 13:11:44.855 [initandlisten]
** WARNING: soft rlimits too low. Number of files is 256, should be at least 1000
> show collections
system.indexes
system.users
test
```

The `db.getCollection`, `count()`, and `findOne()` MongoDB commands will get you rolling:

```
> coll=db.getCollection('test')
fluentd.test
> coll.count()
181
> coll.findOne()
{
    "_id" : ObjectId("5278d9822675c98317000001"),
    "events_flow" : 4,
    "time" : ISODate("2013-11-05T11:41:47Z")
}
```

We leave it to you to learn the MongoDB query syntax and the great aggregation framework. Have fun!

 Fluent has other data store plug-ins, including an Elasticsearch (*http://www.elasticsearch.com*) plug-in that can be very interesting.

6.4. Playing with Basho Riak CS Object Store

CloudStack deals with the compute side of an IaaS cloud by providing management functionalities for virtual machine provisioning. The storage side of a cloud—which often consists of a scalable, fault tolerant object store—is implemented with other software. Ceph (*http://ceph.com/ceph-storage/*) and RiakCS (*http://basho.com/riak-cloud-storage/*) from Basho (*http://basho.com*) are the two of the most talked about object stores these days. In this post, we look at RiakCS and take it for a quick tour. CloudStack integrates with RiakCS for secondary storage, and together they can offer an EC2 and a true S3 interface, backed by a scalable object store.

While RiakCS (*http://basho.com/riak-cloud-storage/*) (cloud storage) can be seen as an S3 backend implementation, it is based on Riak. Riak is a highly available distributed NoSQL database (*http://bit.ly/why_Riak*). The use of a consistent hashing algorithm allows Riak to rebalance the data when nodes disappear (e.g., fail) and when nodes appear (e.g., increased capacity); it also allows you to manage replication of data with an eventual consistency principle typical of large-scale distributed storage systems, which favor availability over consistency.

Problem

You want to use a distributed, scalable object store to act as a storage backend to your image catalog. You want to use RiakCS and get familiar with it on your local machine.

Solution

To get a functioning RiakCS storage, we need Riak, RiakCS, and Stanchion. Stanchion is an interface that serializes HTTP requests made to RiakCS. All three systems can be installed from binaries.

Discussion

To get started, let's play with Riak and build a cluster on our local machine. Basho has some great documentation (*http://bit.ly/5-minute_install*); the toughest thing will be to install Erlang (and by tough I mean a two-minutes deal), but again the docs (*http://bit.ly/Erlang_install*) are very helpful and give step-by-step instructions for almost all operating systems.

There is no need for me to recreate step-by-step instructions, as the docs are so great, but the gist is that with the quick start guide, we can create a Riak cluster on local host. We are going to start five Riak nodes (e.g., we could start more) and join them into a cluster. This is as simple as:

```
bin/riak start
bin/riak-admin cluster join dev1@127.0.0.1
```

Where dev1 was the first Riak node started. Creating this cluster will rebalance the ring:

```
================================= Membership =================================
Status     Ring    Pending    Node
------------------------------------------------------------------------------
valid     100.0%     20.3%    'dev1@127.0.0.1'
valid       0.0%     20.3%    'dev2@127.0.0.1'
valid       0.0%     20.3%    'dev3@127.0.0.1'
valid       0.0%     20.3%    'dev4@127.0.0.1'
valid       0.0%     18.8%    'dev5@127.0.0.1'
------------------------------------------------------------------------------
```

The riak-admin command is a nice CLI to manage (*http://bit.ly/riak-admin_CLI*) the cluster. We can check the membership of the cluster we just created, and after some time, the ring will have rebalanced to the expected state:

```
dev1/bin/riak-admin member-status
================================= Membership =================================
Status     Ring    Pending    Node
------------------------------------------------------------------------------
valid      62.5%     20.3%    'dev1@127.0.0.1'
valid       9.4%     20.3%    'dev2@127.0.0.1'
valid       9.4%     20.3%    'dev3@127.0.0.1'
valid       9.4%     20.3%    'dev4@127.0.0.1'
valid       9.4%     18.8%    'dev5@127.0.0.1'
------------------------------------------------------------------------------
Valid:5 / Leaving:0 / Exiting:0 / Joining:0 / Down:0

dev1/bin/riak-admin member-status
================================= Membership =================================
Status     Ring    Pending    Node
------------------------------------------------------------------------------
valid      20.3%       --     'dev1@127.0.0.1'
valid      20.3%       --     'dev2@127.0.0.1'
valid      20.3%       --     'dev3@127.0.0.1'
valid      20.3%       --     'dev4@127.0.0.1'
valid      18.8%       --     'dev5@127.0.0.1'
------------------------------------------------------------------------------
```

You can then test your cluster by putting an image as explained in the docs and retrieving it in a browser (e.g., an HTTP GET):

```
$ curl -XPUT http://127.0.0.1:10018/riak/images/1.jpg \
     -H "Content-type: image/jpeg" \
     --data-binary @image_name_.jpg
```

Open the browser to *http://127.0.0.1:10018/riak/images/1.jpg*.

As easy as 1, 2, 3!

6.5. Installing RiakCS on Ubuntu 12.04

Problem

To move forward and build a complete S3-compatible object store, you can set up everything on an Ubuntu 12.04 machine. You will need more than one node to really take advantage of the distributed nature of Riak, but starting with one node will put you well on your way.

Solution

Set up the *basho* package repository and use the package manager to grab the *riak*, *riak_cs*, and *stanchion* binaries. Then edit the configuration files and check that you can store an object in RiakCS.

Discussion

To get started, you need to set up the *basho* package repository on your machine. Get the repo keys and set up a *basho.list* repository:

```
# curl http://apt.basho.com/gpg/basho.apt.key | sudo apt-key add -
# bash -c "echo deb http://apt.basho.com $(lsb_release -sc) main \
       > /etc/apt/sources.list.d/basho.list"
# apt-get update
```

Install the `riak`, `riak-cs`, and `stanchion` packages.

```
# apt-get install riak riak-cs stanchion
```

Check that the binaries are in your path with `which riak`, `which riak-cs`, and `which stanchion`; you should find everything in */usr/sbin*. All configuration will be in */etc/riak*, */etc/riak-cs*, and */etc/stanchion*. Make sure to inspect *app.config*, which we are going to modify before starting everything.

Note that all binaries have a nice usage description, which includes a console, a ping method, and a restart, among others:

```
Usage: riak {start | stop| restart | reboot | ping | console | attach |
            attach-direct | ertspath | chkconfig | escript | version |
            getpid | top [-interval N] [-sort reductions|memory|msg_q]
            [-lines N] }
```

Before starting anything, we are going to configure every component, which means editing the *app.config* files in each respective *etc* directory. For `riak-cs`, I only made sure to set `{anonymous_user_creation, true}`; I did nothing for configuring `stanchion`, as I used the default ports and ran everything on `localhost` without `ssl`. Just make sure that you are not running any other application on port `8080` as `riak-cs` will use this port by default. For configuring `riak`, see the documentation (*http://bit.ly/*

configure_Riak), which sets a different backend than what we used in the testing phase. With all these configuration steps complete, you should be able to start all three components:

```
# riak start
# riak-cs start
# stanchion start
```

You can ping every component and check the console with riak ping, riak-cs ping, and stanchion ping.

Create an admin user for riak-cs:

```
# curl -H 'Content-Type: application/json' \
    -X POST http://localhost:8080/riak-cs/user \
    --data '{"email":"foobar@example.com", "name":"admin user"}'
```

If this returns successfully, it is a good indication that your setup is working properly. In the response, we recognized API and secret keys:

```
{"email":"foobar@example.com",
"display_name":"foobar",
"name":"admin user",
"key_id":"KVTTBDQSQ1-DY83YQYID",
"key_secret":"2mNGCBRoqjab1guiI3rtQmV3j2NNVFyXdUAR3A==",
"id":"1f8c3a88c1b58d4b4369c1bd155c9cb895589d24a5674be789f02d3b94b22e7c",
"status":"enabled"}
```

Let's take those and put them in our riak-cs configuration file; there are admin_key and admin_secret variables to set. Then restart with riak-cs restart. Don't forget to also add those in the stanchion configuration file */etc/stanchion/app.config* and restart it stanchion restart.

At this stage, you have a fully functioning RiakCS cluster (one node only), with an administrative user created. You can use the administrator keys to create another user.

6.6. Using Python Boto to Store Data in RiakCS

Problem

RiakCS exposes an S3-compatible API (*http://bit.ly/S3-compatible_API*) and you want to use an S3 client to store and manage objects in RiakCS.

Solution

Use the Python Boto module (Recipe 4.4) to write a Python script that will manage buckets and set some objects in those buckets.

Discussion

Riak-CS is an S3-compatible cloud storage solution, so we should be able to use an S3 client like Python Boto (*http://bit.ly/Boto_docs*) to create buckets and store data. Let's try. You will need Boto of course; `apt-get install python-boto` and then open an interactive shell `python`.

Import the modules and create a connection to `riak-cs`:

```
>>> from boto.s3.key import Key
>>> from boto.s3.connection import S3Connection
>>> from boto.s3.connection import OrdinaryCallingFormat
>>> apikey='KVTTBDQSQ1-DY83YQYID'
>>> secretkey='2mNGCBRoqjab1guiI3rtQmV3j2NNVFyXdUAR3A=='
>>> cf=OrdinaryCallingFormat()
>>> conn=S3Connection(aws_access_key_id=apikey,aws_secret_access_key=secretkey, \
...is_secure=False,host='localhost',port=8080, 
...calling_format=cf)
```

Now you can list the bucket, which will be empty at first. Then create a bucket and store content in it with various keys:

```
>>> conn.get_all_buckets()
[]
>>> bucket=conn.create_bucket('riakbucket')
>>> k=Key(bucket)
>>> k.key='firstkey'
>>> k.set_contents_from_string('Object from first key')
>>> k.key='secondkey'
>>> k.set_contents_from_string('Object from second key')
>>> b=conn.get_all_buckets()[0]
>>> b.get_all_keys()
[<Key: riakbucket,firstkey>, <Key: riakbucket,secondkey>]
>>> k=Key(b)
>>> k.key='secondkey'
>>> k.get_contents_as_string()
'Object from second key'
>>> k.key='firstkey'
>>> k.get_contents_as_string()
'Object from first key'
```

If you want a *riakCS* Boto shell, the following script will be very handy:

```
#!/usr/bin/env python

from boto.s3.key import Key
from boto.s3.connection import S3Connection
from boto.s3.connection import OrdinaryCallingFormat

from IPython.terminal.embed import InteractiveShellEmbed

apikey='C9JEFXWZ5RUFS9U2YZRX'
secretkey='DZ_6jtGC8Any-08YWiKN2vNKPkNxQDmU9rODig=='
```

```
cf=OrdinaryCallingFormat()
conn=S3Connection(aws_access_key_id=apikey,aws_secret_access_key=secretkey,
                  is_secure=False,host='localhost',port=8081,calling_format=cf)

ipshell = InteractiveShellEmbed(banner1="Hello, Riak Shell!")
ipshell()
```

And that's it, an S3-compatible object store backed by a NoSQL distributed database that uses consistent hashing, all of it in Erlang. Pretty sweet. Connect it to your Cloud-Stack EC2-compatible cloud, use it as secondary storage to hold templates, or make it a public facing offering, and you have the second leg of the cloud: a scalable object store.

6.7. Using RiakCS as Secondary Storage for CloudStack

Problem

You have used an NFS storage system as CloudStack secondary storage. Now that you have set up a RiakCS cluster, you want to use it to replace your NFS system.

Solution

Create a CloudStack user in your RiakCS cluster, create a cloudstack bucket that this user can read from and write to. Then use the updateCloudToUseObjectStore API to migrate from NFS to S3-based secondary storage. Alternatively, if you have not set up an NFS secondary storage yet, you can use the addImageStore API to create it with RiakCS.

Discussion

The following steps will migrate from an NFS store secondary storage to an object store.

1. Install and configure a RiakCS cluster per the normal process (Recipe 6.5).
2. Create an access/secret key for a CloudStack user.
3. Configure S3 secondary storage per the CloudStack documentation using the access key and secret key of the RiakCS CloudStack user.

Account management in RiakCS is well described (*http://bit.ly/account_management*). However, to create a user, the s3curl (*http://bit.ly/s3curl_utility*) utility is extremely handy. It will create the proper signature and generate the authenticated request to your S3 endpoint.

Download s3curl (*http://bit.ly/s3curl_utility*) and edit this Perl script to change the endpoint to your RiakCS endpoint. For example, if you run it on *localhost*, edit s3curl to define an endpoint like so:

```
# begin customizing here
my @endpoints = ( 'localhost',);
```

s3curl itself has some good usage info, but the RiakCS documentation (*http://bit.ly/ using_s3curl*) is also very useful.

Using the key_id and the key_secret that you generated in Recipe 6.5, you can list the users:

```
$ ./s3curl.pl --id C9JEFXWZ5RUFS9U2YZRX \
        --key DZ_6jtGC8Any-08YWiKN2vNKPkNxQDmU9rODig== \
        http://localhost:8081/riak-cs/users
```

To create a user, you will need to send some JSON data that contains the name and email of the user (the response will contain the keys of the new user):

```
$ ./s3curl.pl --id C9JEFXWZ5RUFS9U2YZRX \
        --key DZ_6jtGC8Any-08YWiKN2vNKPkNxQDmU9rODig== \
        --post --contentType application/json -- -s -v -x localhost:8081 \
        --data '{"email":"foobar@example.com","name":"foo bar"}' \
        http://localhost:8081/riak-cs/user
```

In order to avoid putting the secret key on the command line, create a *~/.s3curl* configuration file with content similar to the following:

```
%awsSecretAccessKeys = (
    # personal account
    admin => {
        id => 'C9JEFXWZ5RUFS9U2YZRX',
        key => 'DZ_6jtGC8Any-08YWiKN2vNKPkNxQDmU9rODig==',
    },
);
```

Make the file chmod 600, and then the request is simplified.

```
$ ./s3curl.pl --id admin http://localhost:8081/riak-cs/users
```

Note the admin ID being used, instead of the key_id of the administrator user. This new user will be used for CloudStack usage. If you installed CloudStack with NFS-based secondary storage (Recipe 2.3), then use the updatecloudToUseObjectStore API (*http://bit.ly/updateCloudtoUseObjectStore*) to migrate from NFS to your RiakCS-based S3 object store.

Using CloudMonkey, you can make this API call easily:

```
> update cloudtouseobjectstore url=http://localhost:8081/riak-cs
        name=riakcs
        provider=S3
        details[0].key=accesskey
        details[0].value=STU6Z-ZMK1TPMDAXL9I1
        details[1].key=secretkey
        details[1].value=8OuY3mHDXihu0Tdb2aVJ4vuYZLBAl5Z7NiWKsg==
imagestore:
```

```
name = riakcs
id = 6793abce-bebf-4de3-ac9e-7c3a23e3db3d
details:
+-----------+-------------------------------------------+
|   name    |                  value                    |
+-----------+-------------------------------------------+
| secretkey | ecJlaZebrYKj_qYaIfzlRR_1izojGVWjBRFx0Q== |
| accesskey |           ZMJD6-90S2MST4NZMK1Z            |
+-----------+-------------------------------------------+
protocol = http
providername = S3
scope = REGION
url = http://localhost:8081/riak-cs
```

 The provider specified is an uppercase S3; it is case sensitive.

If you want to add an object store in a zone that does not have any existing secondary storage, you could use the addImageStore API like so:

```
> add imagestore
    name=riakcs
    provider=S3
    url=http://localhost:8081/riak-cs
    details[0].key=accesskey
    details[0].value=ZMJD6-90S2MST4NZMK1Z
    details[1].key=secretkey
    details[1].value=ecJlaZebrYKj_qYaIfzlRR_1izojGVWjBRFx0Q==
imagestore:
name = riakcs
id = 1a60d62a-c1e9-4d1c-8b35-d5cd687f6de4
details:
+-----------+-------------------------------------------+
|   name    |                  value                    |
+-----------+-------------------------------------------+
| secretkey | ecJlaZebrYKj_qYaIfzlRR_1izojGVWjBRFx0Q== |
| accesskey |           ZMJD6-90S2MST4NZMK1Z            |
+-----------+-------------------------------------------+
protocol = http
providername = S3
scope = REGION
url = http://localhost:8081/riak-cs
```

This small recipe should put you on your way to using RiakCS with CloudStack.

6.8. Installing Apache Whirr

Apache Whirr (*http://whirr.apache.org*) is a set of libraries to run cloud services, internally it uses jclouds (*http://jclouds.incubator.apache.org*), which we introduced earlier via the `jclouds-cli` interface to CloudStack. It is Java based and of interest to provision clusters of virtual machines on cloud providers. Historically it started as a set of scripts to deploy Hadoop (*http://hadoop.apache.org*) clusters on Amazon EC2. The following recipes introduce Whirr as a potential CloudStack tool to provision Hadoop clusters on CloudStack-based clouds.

Problem

You want to deploy groups of virtual machines that make up a distributed system. Apache Whirr can be used to orchestrate these types of multiple machine deployments.

Solution

Clone the Apache Whirr Git repository and build it using Maven.

Discussion

To install Whirr, you can follow the Quick Start Guide (*http://bit.ly/Whirr_quickstart*), download a tarball, or clone the Git repository. In the spirit of this document, we clone the repo:

```
$ git clone git://git.apache.org/whirr.git
```

And build the source with Maven, which we now know and love:

```
$ mvn install
```

The Whirr binary will be available in the *bin* directory that we can add to our path:

```
$ export PATH=$PATH:/Users/sebgoa/Documents/whirr/bin
```

If all goes well, you should now be able to get the usage of `whirr`:

```
$ whirr --help
Unrecognized command '--help'

Usage: whirr COMMAND [ARGS]
where COMMAND may be one of:

    launch-cluster  Launch a new cluster running a service.
    start-services  Start the cluster services.
     stop-services  Stop the cluster services.
  restart-services  Restart the cluster services.
   destroy-cluster  Terminate and cleanup resources for a running cluster.
  destroy-instance  Terminate and cleanup resources for a single instance.
      list-cluster  List the nodes in a cluster.
```

```
list-providers  Show a list of the supported providers
    run-script  Run a script on a specific instance or
                a group of instances matching a role name
       version  Print the version number and exit.
          help  Show help about an action

Available roles for instances:
  cassandra
  elasticsearch
  ganglia-metad
  ganglia-monitor
  hadoop-datanode
  ...
```

From the look of the usage, you clearly see that Whirr is about more than just Hadoop and that it can be used to configure Elasticsearch clusters and Cassandra databases, as well as the entire Hadoop ecosystem with Mahout, Pig, HBase, Hama, MapReduce, and YARN.

6.9. Using Apache Whirr to Deploy a Hadoop Cluster

Problem

With Whirr installed, you want to configure it so that it can use your CloudStack endpoint to provision virtual machines and deploy a Hadoop (*http://hadoop.apache.org*) cluster.

Solution

Configure Whirr with your CloudStack endpoint and your API keys. Write a properties file that defines the characteristics of the Hadoop cluster you want to start. Your properties file will define the distrubtion of Hadoop you want to use, the number of nodes, the operating system, the instance types, and so on.

Discussion

To get started with Whirr, you need to set up the credentials and endpoint of the CloudStack-based cloud that you will be using. Edit the *~/.whirr/credentials* file to include a PROVIDER, IDENTITY, CREDENTIAL, and ENDPOINT. The PROVIDER needs to be set to cloudstack, the IDENTITY is your API key, the CREDENTIAL is your secret key and the ENDPOINT is the endpoint URL. For instance:

```
PROVIDER=cloudstack
IDENTITY=mnH5EbKc4534592347523486724389673248AZW4kYV5gdsfgdfsgdsfg8...
CREDENTIAL=Hv97W58iby5PWL1ylC4oJls46456435634564537sdfgdfhrteydfg87s...
ENDPOINT=https://api.exoscale.ch/compute
```

With the credentials and endpoint defined, you can create a *properties* file that describes the cluster you want to launch on your cloud. The file contains information such as the cluster name, the number of instances and their type, the distribution of Hadoop you want to use, the service offering ID, and the template ID of the instances. It also defines the SSH keys to be used for accessing the virtual machines. In the case of a cloud that uses security groups, you may also need to specify it. A tricky point is the handling of DNS name resolution. You might have to use the `whirr.store-cluster-in-etc-hosts` key to bypass any DNS issues. For a full description of the Whirr property keys, see the documentation (*http://bit.ly/Whirr_config*).

 To use the Cloudera Hadoop distribution (CDH) like in the preceding example, you will need to copy the *services/cdh/src/main/resources/functions* directory to the root of your Whirr source. In this directory, you will find the bash scripts used to bootstrap the instances. It may be handy to edit those scripts.

```
$ more whirr.properties

#
# Setup an Apache Hadoop Cluster
#

# Change the cluster name here
whirr.cluster-name=hadoop

whirr.store-cluster-in-etc-hosts=true

whirr.use-cloudstack-security-group=true

# Change the name of cluster admin user
whirr.cluster-user=${sys:user.name}

# Change the number of machines in the cluster here
whirr.instance-templates=1 hadoop-namenode+hadoop-jobtracker,
                         3 hadoop-datanode+hadoop-tasktracker

# Uncomment out the following two lines to run CDH
whirr.env.repo=cdh4
whirr.hadoop.install-function=install_cdh_hadoop
whirr.hadoop.configure-function=configure_cdh_hadoop

whirr.hardware-id=b6cd1ff5-3a2f-4e9d-a4d1-8988c1191fe8

whirr.private-key-file=/path/to/ssh/key/
whirr.public-key-file=/path/to/ssh/public/key/

whirr.provider=cloudstack
```

```
whirr.endpoint=https://the/endpoint/url
whirr.image-id=1d16c78d-268f-47d0-be0c-b80d31e765d2
```

 The preceding example is specific to a CloudStack cloud (*http://exos cale.ch*) set up as a basic zone. This cloud uses security groups for isolation between instances. The proper rules had to be setup by hand. Also note the use of `whirr.store-cluster-in-etc-hosts`. If set to true, Whirr will edit the */etc/hosts* file of the nodes and enter the IP adresses. This is handy in the case where DNS resolution is problematic.

You are now ready to launch a Hadoop cluster:

```
$ whirr launch-cluster --config hadoop.properties
Running on provider cloudstack using identity mnH5EbKcKeJd4564...
Bootstrapping cluster
Configuring template for bootstrap-hadoop-datanode_hadoop-tasktracker
Configuring template for bootstrap-hadoop-namenode_hadoop-jobtracker
Starting 3 node(s) with roles [hadoop-datanode, hadoop-tasktracker]
Starting 1 node(s) with roles [hadoop-namenode, hadoop-jobtracker]
>> running InitScript{INSTANCE_NAME=bootstrap-hadoop-datanode_hadoop...
>> running InitScript{INSTANCE_NAME=bootstrap-hadoop-datanode_hadoop...
>> running InitScript{INSTANCE_NAME=bootstrap-hadoop-datanode_hadoop...
>> running InitScript{INSTANCE_NAME=bootstrap-hadoop-namenode_hadoop...
<< success executing InitScript{INSTANCE_NAME=bootstrap-hadoop-datanode_...
Get:1 http://security.ubuntu.com precise-security Release.gpg [198 B]
Get:2 http://security.ubuntu.com precise-security Release [49.6 kB]
Hit http://ch.archive.ubuntu.com precise Release.gpg
Get:3 http://ch.archive.ubuntu.com precise-updates Release.gpg [198 B]
Get:4 http://ch.archive.ubuntu.com precise-backports Release.gpg [198 B]
Hit http://ch.archive.ubuntu.com precise Release
..../snip/.....
You can log into instances using the following ssh commands:
[hadoop-datanode+hadoop-tasktracker]: ssh -i /Users/sebastiengoasguen/.ssh/...
[hadoop-datanode+hadoop-tasktracker]: ssh -i /Users/sebastiengoasguen/.ssh/...
[hadoop-datanode+hadoop-tasktracker]: ssh -i /Users/sebastiengoasguen/.ssh/...
[hadoop-namenode+hadoop-jobtracker]: ssh -i /Users/sebastiengoasguen/.ssh/...
To destroy cluster, run 'whirr destroy-cluster'
with the same options used to launch it.
```

After the bootstrapping process finishes, you should be able to log in to your instances and use Hadoop, or if you are running a proxy on your machine, you will be able to access your Hadoop cluster locally.

## PART IV

Summary

And that's a wrap! We just covered over 20 different tools that have a CloudStack driver or plug-in, or that can be used within a CloudStack infrastructure. There is more, and hopefully this ecosystem will keep on growing to allow you to take full advantage of your cloud. That way, you can move from "How do I build a cloud?" to using it to increase your business agility.

## CHAPTER 7

Summary

What We Covered

We split this book in three parts. Part I covered installation concepts:

- We reviewed the basic requirements to compile CloudStack from source.
- We introduced the simulator, which can be used for testing.
- We introduced DevCloud, a CloudStack sandbox packaged as a VirtualBox image.
- We presented a new project based on Vagrant as an alternative to DevCloud.
- We went through a step-by-step installation from binaries on Ubuntu 14.04 with KVM.

Part II covered clients and API interfaces, including information on how to:

- Sign CloudStack API requests
- Get started with CloudMonkey, the CloudStack CLI
- Use Apache Libcloud
- Use the jclouds command-line interface
- Use CloStack for your Clojure projects
- Use StackerBee for Ruby developers
- Use EC2Stack to provide an EC2-compliant endpoint
- Use Python Boto with EC2Stack
- Use Eutester to write functional tests compatible with AWS EC2 zones
- Use gstack to provide a GCE-compliant endpoint
- Use rOCCI to provide a standard OCCI endpoint

Part III covered configuration management and advanced recipes, including information on how to:

- Get started with Veewee and Packer to create base images for local or cloud use
- Get started with Vagrant and the Vagrant CloudStack plug-in
- Get started with Ansible and how to use it with Vagrant to provision machines in the cloud
- Use the Chef Knife CloudStack plug-in, including bootstrapping instances with Hosted-Chef
- Use fluent to store CloudStack logs
- Get started with RiakCS and how to use it for CloudStack secondary storage
- Use Apache Whirr to provision Big Data solutions

Other Areas to Explore

The CloudStack ecosystem is evolving fast with new tools appearing all the time. For instance, NTT recently developed a CloudFoundry BOSH CPI (*http://bit.ly/BOSH_CPI*) and folks at Klarna (*http://klarna.com*) developed a Packer builder (*http://bit.ly/Packer_builder*) for CloudStack, which hopefully should be merged soon.

If you want to get involved with the CloudStack community, there are several avenues for you to do so:

- Join the mailing lists (*http://bit.ly/CloudStack_mail*) and do not forget to put some filters (otherwise, you might get overwhelmed by the amount of traffic).
- Join the IRC channels on *irc.freenode.net*; developers hang out on *#cloudstack-dev* and users hang out on *#cloudstack*.
- Twitter can be a good source of information about latest development in the ecosystem, so follow the CloudStack community (*@cloudstack*).
- If you use a particular tool and find any issues, you should file a ticket with that project, but you can also file an issue with the CloudStack JIRA instance (*http://bit.ly/CS_JIRA*).

GitHub has become the main source of information for open source software. You can find most if not all of the ecosystem on GitHub:

- Check out the CloudStack mirror (*https://github.com/apache/cloudstack*).
- Most clients are available with the search (*http://bit.ly/search_clients*).

- Some of the tools are also listed under CloudStack extras (*http://bit.ly/ search_clients*).

Final Words

Building a cloud is only a small part of changes happening in IT these days. Architecting and implementing an IaaS offering should be straightforward, and when I see all the CloudStack clouds in production today, I believe it is. We need to start thinking beyond building a cloud and start taking advantage of it. Building a cloud is just one step on our way to changing how we do IT. We need change in application deployments workflow, change in application/resource life cycle, change in the way developers and system administrators operate and use the infrastructure. All that change in the name of business agility.

Amazon Web Services started in 2005/2006 with the now well-known S3 and EC2 services, and they are the building blocks for providing higher level services—from application deployments to data warehousing and real-time processing. The focus should be on providing services and building a vibrant ecosystem. Whether you use CloudStack, OpenStack, Eucalyptus, or OpenNebula should not matter. What should matter is the availability of tools and plug-ins to beef up your arsenal and take advantage of that cloud. Hopefully this book showed you that the CloudStack ecosystem is vibrant, strong, and developing fast. It is driven by users of existing CloudStack deployments who have now moved beyond the design and implementation issues of building a cloud and are now focused on the ecosystem around it to change the way they do IT and have a direct impact on the business mission.

Index

A

addImageStore API, 122
advanced recipes, 109–126
    Apache Whirr, 123
        installing, 123
        using to deploy a Hadoop cluster, 124
    Basho Riak CS object store, 115
        installing RiakCS on Ubuntu, 117
        playing with Riak, 115
        using Boto to store data in RiakCS, 118
        using RiakCS as secondary storage for
            CloudStack, 120
    configuring fluentd CloudStack plug-in, 110
    installing fluentd to collect CloudStack logs
        and events, 109
    using MongoDB as Fluent data store, 113
agents
    configuring libvirt for CloudStack KVM
        agent, 24
    Linux bridge setup for KVM agent, 25
    setting hostname and local DNS names, 23
Amazon Web Services (AWS) API, 34
Ansible, 85
    introducing to configure cloud instances, 95
    playbooks, 91
    provisioning with playbooks, 97
    provisioning with Vagrant CloudStack plug-
        in, 99
Apache Libcloud (see Libcloud)

Apache Whirr, 123–126
    installing, 123
    using to deploy a Hadoop cluster, 124
API clients, 33–63
    Apache Libcloud, 45
        hybrid cloud applications using libcloud,
            49
        installing, 46
        managing key pairs and security groups,
            48
        using IPython interactive shell, 50
    Clojure CloStack, 55
        starting a virtual machine, 59
        using in your own Clojure project, 60
    CloudMonkey
        configuring, 40
        installing, 39
        starting a virtual machine instance, 43
        using as an interactive shell, 42
    CloudStack API, 35
    getting API keys, 36
    jclouds CLI
        installing and configuring, 51
        using with CloudStack, 54
    signing an API request, 37
    StackerBee, Ruby client, 62
API interfaces, 65–82
    adding an AWS EC2 API, 68
    AWS EC2 compliant interface, 65

We'd like to hear your suggestions for improving our indexes. Send email to index@oreilly.com.

133

installing and configuring gstack, 74
supporting OCCI standard in CloudStack, 80
testing AWS compatibility with Eutester, 71
using AWS CLI with EC2Stack, 66
using gstack with gcutil tool, 75
using Python Boto with EC2Stack, 69
availability zones, 27
AWS (Amazon Web Services), vagrant-aws plug-in, 92
AWS EC2 interface to CloudStack, 65
improving EC2Stack API coverage, 68
testing compatibility with Eutester, 71
using Python Boto with EC2Stack, 69

B

Basho Riak CS object store, 115
(see also advanced recipes)
Boto
using to store data in RiakCS, 118
using with EC2Stack, 69

C

CentOS
installing CloudStack prerequisites, 4
installing packages to build CloudStack packages from source, 14
Chef
configuration of NFS and MySQL server and NAT routing, 11
cookbooks, 92
hosted Chef, 105
Knife command-line utility, 102
CIMI (Cloud Infrastructure Management Interface), 80
clients, 33
(see also API clients)
Clojure, 55
using CloStack in your own Clojure project, 60
CloStack, 55
exploring API calls you can make, 58
installing, 57
starting a virtual machine, 59
using in your own Clojure project, 60
cloud providers
libcloud support for, 46
multiple, use with libcloud, 50

cloud, taking advantage of, 131
CloudMonkey
configuring, 40
installing, 39
opening with cloudmonkey command, 40
starting a virtual machine instance with, 43
updateCloudToUseObjectStore API call, 121
using as an interactive shell, 42
using as straightforward CLI, 40
CloudStack, vii
other areas to explore, 130
sandbox (see DevCloud)
using the CloudStack simulator, 7
command line interface (CLI)
jclouds CLI, installing and configuring, 51
using AWS CLI with EC2Stack, 66
using CloudMonkey as, 40
compute offerings, 29
compute service offerings, listing with gcutil, 77
configuration management, 83–108
Ansible
introducing to configure cloud instances, 95
provisioning with Ansible playbooks, 97
provisioning with Vagrant CloudStack plug-in, 99
Knife
installing Knife-CloudStack plug-in, 102
starting an instance with, 104
Packer, using to build cloud images, 88
Vagrant
installing to build and test cloud images, 90
using Vagrant CloudStack plug-in, 92
Veewee
installing, 86
using to create a Vagrant base box, 86
cookbooks, 105
(see also Chef)
CPU overprovisioning factor, 28
create_node method, 48

D

dashboard, Apache CloudStack, 28
databases
MongoDB, using as Fluent data store, 113
Riak NoSQL database, 115
setting up CloudStack database, 20
Debian packages, building, 13

dependencies
    for CloudMonkey, 40
    for CloudStack development, installing, 3
DevCloud, 9
    adding as hypervisor to management server,
        10
    installing prerequisites for, 10
dummy boxes, creating, 93

E

EC2 interface to CloudStack, 65
EC2Stack
    improving API coverage, 68
    installing and configuring, 65
    using AWS CLI with, 66
    using Eutester to write functional tests, 72
    using Python Boto with, 69
Elasticsearch, storing CloudStack logs in, using
    Fluent, 109
Eutester
    installing to test AWS compatibility, 71
    methods available through CloudStack AWS
        EC2 interface, 73
    using with EC2Stack, 72

F

firewalls
    configuring egress firewall rules, 108
    listing with gstack, using gcutil, 78
Flask applications
    EC2Stack, 65
    gstack, 74
Fluent, 109
    configuring fluentd CloudStack plug-in, 110
    installing fluentd to collect CloudStack logs
        and events, 109
    using MongoDB as data store, 113

G

GCE (see Google Compute Engine)
GCE GA v1.0 API, 80
gcutil, 74
    installing and configuring, 76
    using gstack with, 77–80
Git
    Apache CloudStack CloudMonkey reposito-
        ry, 40

Apache CloudStack repository, 6
cloning GSoC-2014, 12
CloudStack ecosystem on GitHub, 130
installing on Ubuntu 14.04, 4
online GitHub tutorial, 6
Google Compute Engine (GCE), 75
    (see also gstack)
    installing and configuring gstack, Cloud-
        Stack GCE interface, 74
Google Compute Engine (GCE) API, 33
Google Summer of Code (GSoC), Vagrant-
    based CloudStack testing deployment, 11
gstack
    installing and configuring, 74
    using with gcutil tool, 75–80

H

Hadoop clusters, 123
    using Apache Whirr to deploy, 124
HMAC (Hashed Message Authentication Code),
    37
hosted Chef, 105
HTTP methods used by CloudStack API, 33
    GET requests, 35
hypervisors
    KVM hypervisor, 15
    preparing a KVM hypervisor, 22
    supported by CloudStack, 22
    using DevCloud to run Xen hypervisors in
        virtualbox image, 9

I

image catalog, setting up and seeding with Sys-
    temVM template, 21
images
    available, listing with gcutil, 77
    building and testing with Vagrant, 90
    building cloud images with Packer, 88
installation
    installing from packages, 15–31
        basic zone network configuration and
            NAT router setup, 25
        configuring a basic zone, 27
        configuring libvirt, 24
        installing prerequisites on management
            server, 17
        preparing a KVM hypervisor, 22

setting up image catalog and seeding it with SystemVM template, 21

setting up management server, 19

troubleshooting your first CloudStack deployment, 30

installing from source, 1–14

building CloudStack from source and running management server locally, 6

building CloudStack packages from source, 13

prerequisites for CentOS 6.5, 4

prerequisites for Unbuntu 14.04, 3

using CloudStack sandbox, DevCloud, 9

using CloudStack simulator, 7

Vagrant-based CloudStack testing deployment, 11

inventory of instances (Ansible), 100

IP address, allocating and associating using Knife, 107

IPv4 forwarding, setting up on management server, 25

IPython

using with Boto, 70

using with Libcloud, 50

J

Java

Java Virtual Machine (JVM), Clojure programming language for, 55

libvirt binding for CloudStack KVM agent, 24

jclouds, 123

jclouds CLI

installing and configuring, 51

using with CloudStack, 54

Jetty, 6

starting new management seerver with simulator profile, 8

K

key pairs

creating SSH key pairs with CloudMonkey, 45

managing SSH key pairs with Libcloud, 48

managing with Knife-CloudStack, 107

keys, API, 36

Knife, 102

starting an instance in the cloud, 104

Knife-CloudStack

installing, 102

listing all available commands, 103

managing key pairs and security groups, 107

pasing list of fields to output, 103

KVM hypervisor

configuring libvirt for CloudStack KVM agent, 24

Linux bridge setup for KVM agent, 25

preparing, 22

setting hostname and local DNS names of agent, 23

KVM-based image, 9

L

Leiningen

installing, 56

using to create a Clojure project skeleton, 60

Libcloud, 45

hybrid cloud applications using, 49

installing, 46

managing key pairs and security groups, 48

using IPython interactive shell with, 50

libmysql-java package, 17

libvirt, configuring for CloudStack KVM agent, 24

list virtualmachines API call, 45

local storage

enabling for compute offerings, 29

using for primary storage, 21

log aggregation framework (see Fluent)

M

machine types, listing with gcutil, 77

management server

installing prerequisites on Ubuntu 14.04, 17

interaction between KVM hypervisor and, 23

setting up, 19

adding community CloudStack repository, 19

database for CloudStack, 20

installing dependencies, 19

setting up IPv4 forwarding on, 25

Marvin, 8

deploying and configuring datacenter, 8

deploying datacenter and configuring for DevCloud hypervisor, 10 installing, 8

Maven
    DevCloud-specific profiles, 10
    installing on Ubuntu 14.04, 4

MongoDB, using as Fluent data store, 113–114

MySQL
    checking status and starting, 5
    installing on Ubuntu 14.04, 4
    service offering table, updating, 31

N

networking
    basic networking zone, 15
    editing network interfaces on management
        server and KVM hypervisor, 17
    network bridge setup, 25

NFS filesystem exported by management server,
    mounting on KVM hypervisor, 22

NFS server, setting up and exporting NFS share
    to hypervisor, 21

NFS store secondary storage, migrating to ob-
    ject store, 120

O

object store, Basho RiakCS, 115

OCCI (Open Cloud Computing Interface), sup-
    porting in CloudStack, 80
    installing rOCCI client, 81
    installing rOCCI server, 80
    testing OCCI client against the server, 82

OGF (Open Grid Forum), 80

OpenJDK, installing on Ubuntu 14.04, 4

overprovisioning factors, 28
    setting in Global Settings, 31

P

packages, 15
    (see also installation, installing from pack-
        ages)
    building CloudStack packages from source,
        13

Packer, 85, 130
    building cloud images, 88

primary storage, 21

public clouds, 74

Python
    creating a API request and signing it, 38

    version 2.7, required by Marvin, 8

Python Boto
    using to store data in RiakCS, 118
    using with EC2Stack, 69

Python management tools, installing, 4

Python Package Index utility (pip)
    installing, 5
    installing Libcloud, 46

Q

query asyncjobresult API call, 45

R

RAM usage of systemVMs, changing, 31

repositories
    community repository for CloudStack pack-
        ages, 13
    creating for CloudStack packages, 13
    setting up management server to use Cloud-
        Stack community repository, 19

Riak, 115

RiakCS, 115
    installing on Ubuntu 12.04, 117
    using as secondary storage for CloudStack,
        120
    using Python Boto to store data in, 118

rOCCI client, installing, 81

rOCCI server, installing and running, 80

Ruby
    Knife-CloudStack, 102
    StackerBee client for CloudStack, 62

S

sandbox (see DevCloud)

secondary storage, 21
    seeding with SystemVM templates, 22
    verifying accessibility, 31

security groups
    creating with CloudMonkey, 45
    creating with gcutil, 78
    managing with Knife-CloudStack, 107
    managing with Libcloud, 49

security policies for libvirt, 24

shells
    CloudMonkey, interactive shell for Cloud-
        Stack, 39
    riakCS Boto shell, 119

using CloudMonkey as interactive shell, 42
using IPython interactive shell with libcloud, 50
simulator profile, building CloudStack with, 8
SSH
    root user to CloudStack deployment, 17
    Vagrant configuration to SSH to an instance, 100
SSH key pairs
    creating with CloudMonkey, 45
    managing with Libcloud, 48
StackerBee, 62
    installing, 63
stop virtualmachine API call, 45
system virtual machines (SVMs)
    changing RAM usage, 31
    seeding image catalog with SystemVM template, 21

T

templates
    building virtual machine templates, 86
    defining local box which references a template in the cloud, 93
tools, new, 130
troubleshooting your first CloudStack deployment, 30

U

Ubuntu
    building CloudStack packages from source, 13
    installing CloudStack prerequisites (version 14.04), 3
updateCloudToUseObjectStore API, 120
updatecloudtoUseObjectStore API, 121

V

Vagrant, 85
    CloudStack plug-in, using with Ansible, 99
    CloudStack testing deployment based on, 11

handling multiple machine definitions, 95
installing to build and test cloud images, 90
provisioning documentation, 92
using Packer to build XenServer Vagrant box, 88
using Vagrant CloudStack plug-in, 92
using Veewee to create a base box, 86
Veewee, 85
    installing, 86
    using to create a Vagrant base box, 86
    Vagrant, 91
virtual machine providers, 86
virtual machine templates, 86
    (see also Veewee)
    building to start Linux distribution ISOs, 86
virtual machines (VMs)
    JVM (Java Virtual Machine), Clojure programming language for, 55
    managing with jclouds CLI, 54
    starting an instance with CloudMonkey, 43
    starting with CloStack, 59
    starting with Libcloud, 48
virtual private clouds (VPCs), 69
VirtualBox
    DevCloud image, 9
    using Veewee with, 86

W

Whirr (see Apache Whirr)
WSGI HTTP servers, 75

X

XenServer Vagrant box, using Packer to build, 88

Z

zones
    basic networking zone, 15
    basic zone network configuration, 25
    configuring a basic zone, 27
    listing availability zones with gcutil, 77

About the Author

Sébastien Goasguen built his first computer cluster while working on his PhD in the late 1990s (when they were still called Beowulf clusters), and he has been working on making computing a utility ever since. He has done research in grid computing and high performance computing, and with the advent of virtualization, moved to cloud computing in the mid 2000s. He is currently a senior open source solutions architect at Citrix, where he works primarily on the Apache CloudStack project, helping develop the CloudStack ecosystem.

Sébastien is a project management committee (PMC) member of CloudStack and Apache Libcloud, and a member of the Apache Software Foundation. He focuses on the cloud ecosystem and has contributed to Knife-cloudstack, Eutester, and Ansible among other open source projects. He is also driving the localization effort of the CloudStack documentation using Transifex and ReadTheDocs.

Colophon

The animal on the cover of *60 Recipes for Apache CloudStack* is a Virginia Northern flying squirrel (*Glaucomys sabrinus fuscus*), a subspecies of the Northern flying squirrel. Related subspecies of flying squirrel are found across North America in Canada and all but the southernmost United States. Mixed and coniferous forests provide suitable habitats for the Northern flying squirrel, which requires generous tree growth for its preferred form of travel.

The flying squirrel does not fly so much as glide, aided in its graceful descent by the patagium, a loose flap of skin stretching between the fore and hind leg on either side of its body. It can launch itself from a treetop from both standing and running positions and adjusts its pitch with a quick flick of its tail to ensure a smooth landing on the trunk of a new tree. Research suggests that the flying squirrel's ability to glide between trees has evolved as a form of locomotion more physiologically economical than movement on all fours across the forest floor.

Flying squirrels are nocturnal and do not hibernate. They have been known to enjoy truffles and other fungi as well as mast. Their living quarters in the cavities of trees are often shared with both relatives and non-relatives.

Many of the animals on O'Reilly covers are endangered; all of them are important to the world. To learn more about how you can help, go to animals.oreilly.com.

The cover image is from Shaw's *Zoology*, vol. 2.1. The cover fonts are URW Typewriter and Guardian Sans. The text font is Adobe Minion Pro; the heading font is Adobe Myriad Condensed; and the code font is Dalton Maag's Ubuntu Mono.

Have it your way.

Get even more for your money.

Join the O'Reilly Community, and register the O'Reilly books you own. It's free, and you'll get:

- $4.99 ebook upgrade offer
- 40% upgrade offer on O'Reilly print books
- Membership discounts on books and events
- Free lifetime updates to ebooks and videos
- Multiple ebook formats, DRM FREE
- Participation in the O'Reilly community
- Newsletters
- Account management
- 100% Satisfaction Guarantee

Signing up is easy:

1. Go to: oreilly.com/go/register
2. Create an O'Reilly login.
3. Provide your address.
4. Register your books.

Note: English-language books only

To order books online:
oreilly.com/store

For questions about products or an order:
orders@oreilly.com

To sign up to get topic-specific email announcements and/or news about upcoming books, conferences, special offers, and new technologies:
elists@oreilly.com

For technical questions about book content:
booktech@oreilly.com

To submit new book proposals to our editors:
proposals@oreilly.com

O'Reilly books are available in multiple DRM-free ebook formats. For more information:
oreilly.com/ebooks

9 781491 910139